Postmark Baghdad

✦

On Patrol with the Iraqi National Police

LTC Matthew K. Green

iUniverse, Inc.
New York   Bloomington

Postmark Baghdad

On Patrol with the Iraqi National Police

iUniverse books may be ordered through booksellers or by contacting:

iUniverse
1663 Liberty Drive
Bloomington, IN 47403
www.iuniverse.com
1-800-Authors (1-800-288-4677)

ISBN: 978-0-595-50818-1 (pbk)
ISBN: 978-0-595-50878-5(cloth)
ISBN: 978-0-595-61663-3 (ebk)

Printed in the United States of America

Dedication

To Alexandria and Olivia who waited patiently: May you too find the gifts of Hope, Harmony, Happiness, and Home.

Contents

Table of Figures

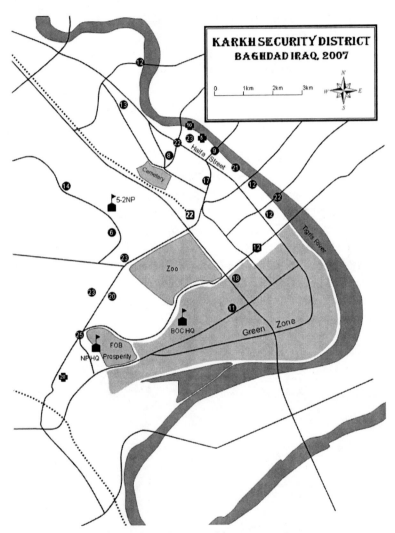

Figure 1: Map of the Karkh Security District

Places of Interest

Numbered by chapter

- 5 Leka Maternity Hospital
- 6 Trash River
- 8 The Egyptian
- 9 Adnon Statue
- 10 Clinic
- 11 Mortar Attack
- 12 Fish Market
- 12 Café suicide vest
- 12 Illegal booze stands
- 12 Destroyed Bridge
- 13 Paper Boy
- 14 LT Mahmoud's Car Bomb
- 17 Alawi Market
- 18 Iraqi Parliament
- 20 Yarmook Hospital
- 20 Kindi Market Car Bomb
- 21 Swim meet
- 22 7th Imam March bridge
- 22 Baghdad Train Station
- 22 7th Imam aid station
- 23 Old Intelligence HQ raid
- 23 Old woman's house
- 23 Yarmook Gas Station massacre
- 25 Black Water traffic Circle incident

Figure 2: Index to Places of Interest

Introduction

I remember sitting and staring at the computer screen for several minutes. The email from the armor branch assignments officer contained a new set of orders and a variety of other attachments that would explain how my life was about to change. It was not so much the news that I would be heading back to Iraq that had sent a shock through my system—I had spent the last year training to go back—rather it was the task I was being assigned to do. "Major Green, you have been selected to be the Team Chief for a National Police Transition Team going to Iraq in January of 2007. You will proceed to Fort Riley, Kansas in October 2006 to attend three months of predeployment training."

"Why in the world would they pick me to do this?" Training foreign forces was not my specialty. I had spent most of my early career with tanks. My recent military education at the Army's Command and General Staff College and later in the School of Advanced Military Studies was focused primarily on moving whole divisions and corps around, not leading a small tactical team or forming and training units. I did not speak Arabic. I was not a Special Forces officer or a Foreign Area Officer. I certainly had no experience in anything remotely like police work. "What were they thinking?"

Eventually my brain unlocked and I wrapped it around the problem. The army was starting to put into place the policies that would eventually become the strategy that is now routinely referred to as "The Surge." While most people associate The Surge with an expanded presence of five extra brigades totaling about 30,000 troops, which deployed to Iraq for most of the duration of 2007 and into early 2008, several other important changes accompanied the increase in raw combat power. The one that was about to become the most important to me was the Transition Team Program.

For several years, the Army had been working to stand up new Iraq Security Forces after disbanding the Saddam era Iraqi Army. The new forces would have a national identity and were a vital step in making Iraq a sovereign nation once again. To do so, the American Army and Marine Corps had been creating ad hoc teams of advisors and trainers to work with Iraqi units: training them and getting them the equipment they needed. There was very little standardization across the process. Some units put their best and brightest against the task—others did not. To solve the problem the Army was starting to centralize the process. Over the next few years, hundreds of eleven man teams would form, conduct a standard core-training curriculum, and then move into theater to link up with an Iraqi Battalion, Brigade, or Division staffs.

Our mission statement was relatively simple. Train, coach, and mentor your Iraqi counterparts and help them form the most effective units they can. That was a wide-open charter. As I thought about it, that really was the same charter I had all along—in every unit that the Army had assigned me to. From my very first tank platoon in Operation Desert Storm to commanding a tank company in Georgia, to being the executive officer of a cavalry squadron, my responsibilities had always largely been the same: Train, coach and mentor the soldiers in my unit and make them the most effective that they could be. For that task, I was certainly well prepared. So the question stopped being "why me?" and turned quickly into "why not me?"

As I began reading the documents attached to the email, I was generating more questions than answers. Answers that, looking back, I know now could not possibly have been answered effectively. The simple fact is that each team that deployed faced a very different set of problems and our stories and experiences are incredibly diverse. Some teams would spend the bulk of their time trying to raise a unit from scratch. They labored to help recruit forces and obtain weapons and vehicles. Others got to their units after they had been formed but before they were ready to fight. They would focus on marksmanship, and leadership and small unit training. Some of us joined units that were already veterans of Iraq's harshest battles: Fallujah or Ramadi, or out in Al Anbar. Some teams found themselves alone and isolated, living bleak and lonely tours as the only Americans in Iraq's farthest reaches. Others found ourselves living in the most well supplied bases in the heart of Baghdad. For some the war became all about local tribal politics and revolved around the Sunni insurgency. For others the fight revolved around the Shia Militias, government corruption, and the swirling national level politics of Baghdad. Some teams would experience far more than their share of improvised explosive devices (IEDs) and combat. Others found local politics and rebuilding infrastructure and economies to be the most time consuming tasks. All of us found that we would become the link between the Iraqi units and American units. A necessary partnership, if we were ever to reach a solution.

I had no idea as I read those first documents where my journey was going to lead. It eventually took me to the 5th Brigade of the Iraqi National Police—"the Sword Brigade" operating in the heart of Baghdad, the Karkh district. The Iraqi National Police Force was a little over a year old at the time. It had been created by banding together a collection of military organizations that had grown up during the previous years in support of the interim government. The Commando Battalions and Public Order Battalions were all merged into one command organized under the Minister of the Interior. The total force consisted of eight brigades organized into two divisions and a few other separate battalions. They were largely stationed in Baghdad and provided, to some extent, a balance of power between the Minister of Defense and the Minister of the Interior.

The early history of the National Police was checkered at best. The units owed allegiance to a variety of political masters. They had been hastily formed and lacked any formal training programs for either the officers or non-commissioned officers who led them. They had chronic supply problems and were armed with a hodge-podge of cast off equipment and uniforms. In a very real sense, they were an armed mob. Where they had some decent leaders they performed adequately, but, in most cases, they were part of the problem and in very many cases were actively engaged in supporting the various militias.

What I would eventually find was that the Sword Brigade was relatively typical of the National Police at the time. Like most brigades across the world's armies, it consisted of about 2500 soldiers—or in this case policemen or "shurta". The brigade had a Brigade Headquarters Staff, a Commando Company and three subordinate battalions of about 750 shurta each. The battalions were essentially equipped as light infantry with an AK-47 automatic rifles being the standard weapon and one of several Soviet era machine guns and a few rocket propelled grenades (RPGs) mixed in to give them a bit more offensive punch. They drove a disparate collection of up-armored pickup trucks—typically Chevy Silverado or Ford F150s with armor plates bolted on the sides and a pintle-mount for a machine gun welded in the floor bed of the back. They had just enough radios to perform rudimentary command and control and we had given them a few specialty vehicles: an ambulance, a wrecker and a few fuel trucks. In many cases, their enemy outgunned them.

When I landed in Baghdad almost six months later, that was about the extent of what I knew. Over the spring of 2007, I would learn that my job as advisor would include any number of other things: role model, negotiator, trophy wife, bail bondsman, private detective, city planner, friend and writer.

That final role is maybe the one that surprised me the most. I had never really considered myself as a writer nor had I suspected I had much talent for it. However, I am an historian by education and I felt some responsibility to document what I was doing. I began writing home a series of letters to friends and family. It became clear early on that there was a huge desire among those at home to hear the other side of the story—the side the mainstream news media just could not seem to capture. Over time, those letters and the dialog they generated with countless friends, both old and new, became therapeutic for me. This book is a collection of those letters. They have been edited slightly for grammar and punctuation but otherwise I have left them largely intact.

Because they were written at the time, and not written to be published as a set, there are some challenges with binding them into a coherent whole. The first, and most notable one, is that I did not write them with any grand thesis or agenda to prove. Looking back, the reader will almost certainly be able to draw several of the same conclusions that I ended up reaching. I was often surprised to see my own impressions and attitudes about Iraq, its people, and the war change in a variety of ways. As I wrote I tried to be cognizant that I was only seeing one small part of the picture, and it is dangerous to draw larger conclusions from such a small sample. I hope that the images and stories I tell here will help merge with the reader's other experiences and allow them to draw their own conclusions. It is certainly not my intention to sell you on mine.

The letters were written as the story unfolded. In most cases, they were distributed via email to friends and family within several days of events actually happening on the ground. Writing from a combat zone has some risks to it. Everything I wrote took into account the requirement for operational security, and in many cases for the privacy of the men on my team. I have gone back and added some of the proper names that were originally omitted. Nevertheless, an astute reader will note that in most cases I have been vague on many of the specifics of names or places. That was intentional then, and is intentional now. What I hope to give the reader is a diary—a look into the ideas and observations, the hopes and frustrations of the moment. Others can go back and reconstruct the facts, the dates, and the numbers. They can clean up the history if they choose. I do not.

I look back now on my first shocked reactions in front of the computer and laugh. The initial dread at being assigned to the Transition Team task has long since faded. It is replaced by gratitude for an experience that was one of the most professionally rewarding of my career, and laced with some of the most profound personal experiences as well. Countless friends and family have encouraged me to make those experiences part of the public record. So here they are—thirty letters home—postmarked Baghdad.

Update #1: 5 January 2007— Memory Lane

My sense that history is repeating itself has been strong lately. Early last week, Mom and Dad met me for breakfast on a clear cold day at Fort Riley, Kansas, where I have been training for the last three months. They were there to pick up my car and say goodbye as I leave for yet another trip to Iraq. As we drove down I-70, we reminisced at the landmarks. There were many.

To the right stood the hangars where I returned from Desert Storm and reunited with my fiancé. A mile later, the Dreamland Motel, where she and I stayed that first night back (and interestingly, the place Timothy McVeigh stayed the night before bombing the Oklahoma Federal Building). A bit further down stood the hotel where Mom and Dad stayed the night after they got married. A few blocks further sat the motel where I stayed when Dad dropped me off years earlier as I signed into my first unit as a brand new Second Lieutenant—just days before deploying to Desert Storm. Through the gate and onto main post, Dad ticked off the landmarks of his first days in the Army and his similar trip to Vietnam with the First Infantry Division—The Big Red One. We bypassed Custer Hill where I spent my first happy years in the Army back in the early 90's, and finally arrived back at Camp Funston, where I have been training. Going back almost 100 years, Camp Funston happens to be the same place where my great

1

grandfather served as a doctor in the training camps deploying soldiers to WWI.

If history is going to keep cycling on me, I see no reason not to revive the task of writing my now infamous "weekly updates." I first penned that series of fifteen letters almost two years ago, in what started as an efficient way to keep friends and family up to date. It turned into rather more. The address list began at about twenty and grew to well over a hundred, with untold numbers of forwarded copies ending up in surprising places. Both the act of writing and the responses became therapeutic. Many have suggested that I write a blog this time—they are very popular. We shall see. I would rather keep it a bit more personal than that.

I will start by saying that I did a poor job of keeping up with many of you in the intervening few years since my last messages. Life at home gives far less time to reflect I suppose. So to catch folks up a bit: I returned home from Mosul, Iraq, late in 2004, just before the first Iraqi national elections. We were optimistic back then. While there was still plenty of fighting, we felt we were on the downhill stretch, and it looked as if democracy had a real hope of taking root. My unit, 1-14th Cavalry felt very proud of what we had done there. We returned to Fort Lewis for a well-deserved rest, and in the way of the Army, the unit split apart. By early spring, we had about a sixty percent turnover of our soldiers and about an eighty percent turnover of our officers. I continued to serve as the S3 operations officer until June and then moved up into the executive officer job. When the unit completely recovered and rested, we embarked on a demanding year-long training program that would bring the squadron back to Iraq in July of 2006. The Army had me slated to deploy again with the unit, but in a series of unforeseen events, I was pulled from the unit about six weeks before they deployed. It was a particularly hard blow, as I felt considerable remorse at sending the unit back into harm's way while I stayed behind. Over the next two months, the Army changed my orders something like six times, significantly adding to my frustration.

For those who follow such things, summer of 2006 was about the time the Army decided to put a renewed emphasis on training Iraqi units by embedding teams of U.S. advisors. I was ripe for the picking and found myself assigned to the task. So now, as a newly promoted Lieutenant Colonel, I commanded a team of eleven soldiers that advises and trains an Iraqi National Police Brigade in the heart of

Baghdad. I imagine we will all have a better idea of what that really means as these letters unfold.

What it has meant for the last few months is a frustrating stint away from my wife and daughters while the team was formed, equipped, trained, and otherwise probed and prodded into a real unit. I will describe the team more in subsequent letters. For now, suffice it to say that most of us will spend a total of sixteen to eighteen months of our lives on this endeavor, with a year of it in country. We are all very glad to have finally arrived in Kuwait and have our twelve-month clock start.

As new and challenging as the training team mission will be, the physical acts of getting to country have been as familiar and timeless as ever. Departure was somewhat easier in that we had all left our families behind, scattered across the country when we returned from a short Christmas break. While the last few hours were touched with cell phone conversations, much of the emotion had already been spent. In the way soldiers do, the last day passed endlessly packing, repacking, checking, repacking, sorting, and stacking bags and kit to relieve stress. We all did it ... we joked about it ... and then continued to fiddle.

One of the more fascinating transitions is that of the contents of my pockets. First casualty is the keys. Car keys pass on to Dad early in the day; the only survivor is the universal key for the four locks on the duffle bags that now constitute my worldly possessions. It is moved to the dog tag chain, along with two silver tags, a cross, and a red allergy alert tag. I have to replace the keys with something ... how about a lucky stone? A little superstition cannot hurt, can it? The wallet gets a good cleaning. Will not be seeing ATM or credit card receipts for awhile ... damn, that last steak and beer were good ... should have had another. Costco card ... out. Frequent flyer card ... out. Note to do this or that ... oops ... did not get around to it ... out. Business cards ... tuck all that into a little baggy for resurrection later. Wow, this wallet got thin! But no worries, my Uncle will take care of me. We land and are showered with a host of new cards: rules of engagement card, basic Arabic phrases, medevac request card, pay and allowances card, uniform standards and do not forget safety. Ahhh, much more comforting to have a fat wallet again!

The cell phones have all been turned off and stored. The plane is strangely quiet without the constant background of ring tones and text messages. Every now and then a ghost vibration or sound will convince you that you have a call, but that is all pure fancy now. We all get a chuckle when we see one of our mates suffer the phantom ring.

Even the coins will eventually change form. I hit the PX[1] earlier to pick up some shaving cream. They do not give coins as change in the PX. Instead, they give out little cardboard funny money discount coupons called POGs. I have no clue what that stands for. So now, I have a curious mix of money and paper coins. My grandfather warned me "not to take any wooden nickels." These are paper, so I hope I will be OK.

The reception camps in Kuwait are much the same as I remember them. Sadly, I have now in-processed here more than any other assignment in my career. Sometimes I think winning the Cold War was not such a good idea. Soldiering in Europe seemed much more glamorous when I was growing up and living there with my father.

Between the deserts in Yakima, Washington, New Mexico (where I spent two months patrolling the border last year), the National Training Center at Fort Irwin, California, and the sands of Kuwait and Iraq, I will go on record as having nothing at all good to say about the desert. Some folks claim a beauty, that if I ever saw, I can no longer recognize; probably because the grit in my teeth, the hang nails of dehydrated skin, and the labored breathing caused by dust all serve to remind me at every turn that the desert is not your friend.

I will cut this short for now. It will be several more weeks until I get consistent and reliable internet and a place where I can write without the distractions of sixty other people crowded into a tent. I will tell you more about my team next week. They are an interesting bunch, and I feel lucky to have gotten this particular group.

---

[1]   The PX or Post Exchange sells services and consumer goods to military members and their families on military bases and to deployed troops.

Figure 3: Pre-deployment Training at Fort Riley Kansas. Top: Sergeant First Class Carrejo, Major Koast, Staff Sergeant Pettus, Sergeant First Class Babb, Staff Sergeant Ethington, Major Brede. Bottom: Captain Szkotnicki, Sergeant First Class Sartin, Lieutenant Colonel Green, Captain Ly, Sergeant First Class King

Update #2: 20 January 2007—Roll Call

The C130 touched down at Baghdad International Airport so gracefully that even the salty old veterans failed to notice we had landed. Years of practice by the pilot, I suppose. I cannot help but wonder how many flights the pilot has made and how many more the nation will ask of him. That observation can be made of almost all the activity I have observed over the last few days both in Kuwait and now in Iraq. You get the overwhelming sense that everyone has done this before, and indeed, most have. Two years ago, I had a sense that procedures were new and there was a distinct and palatable taste of anxiety as folks arrived into theater. That is gone, and even the very newest recruits seem to be buoyed by the veterans to their left and right. We have been at this a long time now, and regardless of your individual perspective on the merit of what has been achieved, the experience earned between the Tigris and Euphrates will pay dividends to our military for decades to come. But, I digress.

We land just after dark, and while it is not raining, everything is wet. Hard to say how long it has been since it did rain. It may have been days. This time of year, the water just pools everywhere and stagnates. It mixes into the sand creating muddy pools the consistency of watery cement. Wooden catwalks take you from place to place. The temperature is chilly, but not as cold as it was in Kuwait. I had expected it to be colder.

We shuffle off the plane and over to the baggage truck to pick our rucksacks out of the pile. We are all already loaded down with weapons, body armor, helmets, our assault packs and, in most cases, a computer case. When we weighed in for the flight, I was carrying just over a hundred pounds of gear. Add to that our rucksacks, and we would all spend the next few hours lugging around about a hundred and sixty pounds - fun, fun, fun. Whenever I do the duffle bag drag, and the back begins to protest, I think back to the Roman legions dragging ninety pounds of kit. Most of them were barely five foot tall, and carved out an empire wearing sandals! Or, the soldiers in the American Civil War doing it all in wool pants and crappy shoes ... if they had shoes at all. I would like to tell you that that helps, but when I finally drift back to reality, all I can think is "Damn, my back hurts!"

We shuffle into a CH47 Chinook helicopter (a school bus size airship with two rotors) for the final leg of this stage of our journey. One more week of training at a special academy for the training teams awaits us. I had never ridden in a Chinook before. The event was much like a ride at Disney Land ... fun, but I am still not sure it was worth the wait in line (did I mention that the back hurt?) By now it is about 8 p.m. and pitch black outside, which really struck me as odd given that we were essentially in the middle of the nation's capital. Baghdad is a big city. You would expect the ambient glow that fills the sky of most major cities. The sort of luminous bubble you can see for miles away on the horizon. I have often thought that that glow indicated the personality of a town. You cannot help but drive up to a city like Las Vegas, Tokyo, or New York and wonder what delights you might find in that dome of light!

Poor old Baghdad had almost no glow. At first, I thought I was just not seeing it. Maybe the lights of the airport were distorting my perspective. As we took off to the north, serenaded by the rhythmic tattoo of the rotors, it was clear that there simply were not a lot of lights to be seen. I imagine the combined effects of a curfew (no cars equals no headlights) and power distribution problems (I have no basis to judge success or failure in this regard) both play a part. My guess is that most of the lights I did see were related to one Coalition Force activity or another. If Baghdad had ever had an enticing glow in its youth, I do not know. If it did, it is gone. "Visitors not welcome," the old man cries.

Nevertheless, visitors Baghdad has. Tonight, twenty-eight training teams have arrived ready to disperse across the city. I promised to tell you a bit about my team last week, so here goes. Each team consists of eleven members whose exact skill sets vary by the type of unit we will train and whose rank varies by the echelon we will train. In my case, we will be training an Iraqi National Police brigade. As a brigade team, I will have three subordinate teams working under me with associated battalions. We do not have an equivalent of "National Police" in the U.S. They are not your average beat cop, and in most cases do not do much in the way of law enforcement. They are probably much closer to the Italian Carabinieri or our National Guard when working for a state governor.

The team is, of course, led by yours truly. I will spare you any further introduction. I have two majors. The first, Major Kyle Brede is my deputy. He is an aviator by trade (flew Chinooks and Guardrail, so was like a kid in a candy shop last night). A jovial Texan, every time we arrive at a new location he proclaims loudly "I ain't ever been to this part of Texas before!" His partner in crime is my operations officer Major Scott Koast. He is a military policeman hailing from New Jersey and brings a solid record of training detainee operations. Major Koast is significantly more stoic than Major Brede but has a razor sharp wit. Together they remind me of Ernie and Burt from *Sesame Street*. Interestingly when Major Brede finds a topic that he is dead serious about, they flip flop rolls, and Burt becomes Ernie. Both are prior service, having served some enlisted time before commissioning. That makes the three of us about the same age in spite of my being several years senior in rank. They both have previous tours in Iraq. It makes for a very easy working relationship.

I have two junior captains, both in their mid-twenties. My logistics officer, Captain Hung Ly, was born in Vietnam and immigrated to Florida as a young boy. Blessed with a quick mind and a great sense of humor, he takes a significant amount of guff over his tiny stature, but dishes out grief in equal measure. With a combat tour two years ago, he brings experience beyond his years. I expect he will be the one to "go native" and learn Arabic the fastest. The other captain, John Szkotnicki, is my intelligence officer. A die-hard Pittsburg Steelers fan, he spent his first few years in the Army as an infantry lieutenant, and has now switched branches. If I have any complaints about how the Army has staffed or equipped these teams, it would be how badly the intelligence community has done giving us folks with any experience. Fortunately, John is a smart kid and will make up in determination what the Army has failed to provide him in experience.

I should mention that all of my officers are active duty, as is the first of my non-commissioned officers. Sergeant First Class Lester Carrejo is my communications NCO. With over twenty years in the Army, he brings a wealth of experience, much of it with combat tours with the 82nd Airborne. A Hispanic-American from Texas, Sergeant First Class Carrejo is often the one to break tension with a timely joke, usually at his own expense.

My medic, Staff Sergeant Jeffrey Ethington (aka Doc or Junior) is our baby, aging in at twenty-three and hailing from Wisconsin. Junior is our only unmarried soldier, and is theoretically attending the University of Wisconsin, but is now on his second tour in Iraq, which puts him on a year-on-year-off school schedule. A trained Emergency Medical Technician in civilian life, he comes to us from the Army Reserve. Blessed with the energy of youth, and a light heart, Doc is the golden retriever of the group. Much to my delight, he is also a fantastic medic and in every exercise rose to the top of the class. Needless to say, we are all glad for it.

The remaining four NCOs are all infantryman from the Army Reserves or National Guard, specifically one of the training support divisions that run basic and officer training for the reserves. Most come to us from Drill Sergeant assignments held prior to joining the team.

Sergeant First Class Michael Babb from North Carolina is a full time guardsman, with prior service in the 82nd in Desert Storm. Possessing a caustic wit and drive to get things done, Sergeant First Class Babb is a workhorse in the group.

Sergeant First Class Gary Sartin is also an old 82nd guy from Desert Storm days and is now my team's senior NCO. A bit of a romantic, we often kid him about pictures of sunsets he sends home to Alabama. I have noticed that some of the others have quietly copied his photos onto their hard drives.

Sergeant First Class Wendell King comes from rural South Carolina. A quiet African-American with some active duty time in

Germany early in his career, he is our old man at forty-nine. He has a belly laugh that starts at his toes and rolls up out of him and does not stop until the entire group is chuckling.

Finally, Staff Sergeant Ashley Pettus is a mechanic from South Carolina. He spent several years on active duty as a helicopter crew chief and then went into the reserves as a drill sergeant, a job he loves, and at which, I know he excels. I cannot wait to unleash him on the Iraqis. We are looking forward to the birth of his first child this spring.

That is a typical representative cross-section of the Army. I will say that compared to most of the other teams I feel extraordinarily blessed with the density of combat veterans and especially recent Iraq veterans that I have on the team. Most of the other teams are lucky to have one or two, and in most cases, it is not the team leader. For whatever reason our team came together very quickly and has had a tame forming-storming-norming-performing cycle. I attribute that to two things. First, I had just spent two years either in combat or in training a unit to go back, so I was intimately familiar with most of the tasks we were required to train over the last few months. Because I was not anxious about the training, and some of the unusual situations we found ourselves in, neither were they. That was not always the case to the left and right of us, as teams often had no idea what right looked like, or why a task needed to be trained at all. Context is important, but not always provided. Second, this group of eleven soldiers is possessed with a gift of sarcasm that even I have a hard time keeping up with. Further, they have an ability to laugh at themselves, which is, quite frankly, unusual. I have no illusions that life in a micro-society will be easy, but this is as good a group to be caged up with as I could have hoped for. All that is left is to see if the Iraqis I am given offer as much promise.

As we draw closer to finally arriving at our new home and actually getting to work, I have spent more time contemplating what the Iraqi commander I will be assigned will be like. We have been through class after class on Arab culture, and the importance of building a personal relationship, and every intricacy of values differences and religious nuances. I cannot escape the almost absurd conclusion that my entire job for the next year is to enter into an "arranged marriage" and see if I can manage the house from the inside. An arranged marriage! What a horrible thing to contemplate. My entire ability to succeed or fail, and indeed to enjoy myself or be miserable for the next year, will in large measure be tied to how well I can get along with someone I have never met and have absolutely no say in picking. It is very possible that I will get a real patriot. I met a variety of Iraqi army officers during my last tour that had amazing stories and were risking everything to do the right thing. However, for every good one, there were a host of other products of nepotism who had no business commanding anything. Sadly, the National Police has a history of corruption, so I am expecting more of the latter. We shall see.

Nothing left to do, I guess, but close for now and get to work. I must have something blue around here somewhere...

Figure 4: Major Kyle Brede 5-2NPTT XO (left), and Major Tom Weiss, Black Jack Brigade's Iraqi Security Forces Officer (right)

Figure 5: Major Scott Koast at Fort Riley, Kansas.

Figure 6: Captain Hung Ly at Forward Operating Base Liberty

Figure 7: Captain John Szkotnicki at Muthana Airfield

Figure 8: Sergeant First Class Lester Carrejo at the 5-2 National
Police Headquarters

Figure 9: Staff Sergeant Jeffrey Ethington "DOC" at FOB Prosperity

Figure 10: Sergeant First Class Michael Babb on C-130 Flight from Kuwait to Baghdad

Figure 11: Sergeant First Class Gary Sartin at FOB Justice

Figure 12: Sergeant First Class Wendell King at FOB Prosperity

Figure 13: Staff Sergeant Ashley Pettus at FOB Prosperity

Update #3: 23 January 2007— Arrival

"Sir, your flight will be here in fifteen minutes, you need to get your team's bags loaded up ASAP. Two other teams are going out with you, so pack it in!"

I chuckled, we were not supposed to load up and head for the airfield for another two hours. It was at least a fifteen-minute bus ride from where we had spent the final week of our training at a small base outside of Baghdad. We piled out of the decrepit Iraqi barracks that used to house the much-celebrated Republican Guard, and into the rain. We raced to load four duffle bags and a rucksack onto the trucks and sped off into the night. A pair of UH-60 helicopters would take us back south to our new home. I looked forward to a view of the city as we flew back in, but was sorely disappointed. The Blackhawk is a much smaller bird than the Chinook, and a pair of the birds was barely enough to hold our kit. The crew chiefs packed most of our baggage onto one bird, eleven men on the second, and all the rest of the bags on top of us. The bags reached the ceiling and I spent the next fifteen minutes staring at a wall of canvas and listening to the changing pitch of the rotors as we sped south.

We touched down at the small airstrip of an Iraqi compound, quickly downloaded our kit from the birds, and then watched them depart gracefully in a whirl of dust and debris. From the edge of the field emerged the team we would replace. We had never met these eleven men, but you would have thought we were long lost brothers based on the smiles on their faces. Our arrival being the long-awaited evidence they needed to truly believe that their year in country was finally drawing to a close. They were a bit surprised that we too were upbeat and excited. We have been at this now for almost four months, so find ourselves glad to get started!

Part of the welcoming committee included Barney, a white and brown dog of unknown breed who apparently has made it a point to guard the American portion of the base. He sniffed us all, registering us in his database. Word is that he does not like Iraqis much and gets very vocal if any strangers move in and about our living quarters. He has apparently been spayed by the vet and gets regular shots and checkups. Pets are normally against the rules, so I was a bit surprised that Barney is allowed to stay. Needless to say, everyone instantly fell in love with him.

Our counterparts scoop us up, whisk us away to our respective living quarters, and begin chatting away eagerly. Mercifully, my counterpart understands that we have plenty of time, so the work waited until the morning. Daylight provided our first good look at our new home, and it takes only a short time to visit ever corner of our tiny Forward Operating Base[2]. I will not complain. About three hundred Americans occupy a smattering of old Iraqi buildings and the trailers that have replaced tents or the old Quonset huts that were so popular a generation ago. Tucked in along the Tigris River, the FOB is blessed with an abundance of palm trees, so while there is no mistaking that you are living in a dirty desert, there is shade and the palms make it almost cheerful. I went for a run around the perimeter yesterday—shocking to some of you, I know! You have to do several laps to generate any distance. I was pleasantly surprised at the smell of pine trees on the backside. A small grove is just enough to take me back to where my children live near Seattle; if I close down all the other senses.

---

[2]   The Forward Operating Base or FOB has become the center of activity of military forces forward deployed in Iraq and Afghanistan. Essentially a military city, it provides a relatively safe haven from which units operate. Part of "The Surge" strategy was to get units off the FOBs and out into more direct contact with the population. To do so, a whole host of smaller Combat Outposts (COPs) and Joint Security Stations (JSSs) were established.

Over the next week we ventured out into the city and over to the larger FOBs. They have grown into sprawling cities with a staggering array of living trailers, motor pools, mess halls, Post Exchanges and fast food stands. The bases are like huge anthills, churning with activity and discharging working parties out into the streets of Baghdad in steady streams. Convoys march around the city on one task or another, all eventually returning to the colony. I, for one, prefer the smaller FOB. Mail only comes once a week, the chow is not as good or varied, we have no PX, but it is much more likable.

The team has grown from eleven to sixteen. One Department of Justice civilian, a law enforcement expert, who is theoretically here to help us train police-like processes, joins us. Given that the National Police do not do normal police work, his exact role is a bit of a mystery. But it is good to have an extra gun on the team when we hit the street, and we are glad to have him. We have picked up our four "terps"—local Iraqi translators. Gary is in his late twenties and is a trained doctor. Unfortunately, he can make about ten times more translating English than he does in an Iraqi hospital. His family is not at all happy that he is working with us. He hopes to get a U.S. Visa. Rafid is also in his late twenties and has been a terp for almost three years. A newlywed and a non-practicing Muslim, he is making the best of the chaotic conditions. Saki is in his late forties. A civil engineer by trade, he is an Armenian Christian. I have not gotten to spend much time with him yet. Finally, Victor is the young man of the bunch. Also trained as an engineer, he is eager to please and very ambitious. Because there is a large concentration of training teams on this FOB, there are many other terps. They form an interesting sub-culture, not purely Iraqi, but also not American. They bridge the gap with the rest of the FOB's Iraqi population, a collection of shop keepers, laundry workers, janitors, cooks, barbers, etc. who all chose to risk persecution for the quality of life that service with the Americans provides.

By now, you are all certainly dying to know how the "wedding" went. Well, I had a bit of a scare. Major General Karim is, quite simply, the largest Iraqi I have ever seen. Tall and fat, the first image that went through my mind was of Jabba the Hut! I quickly dropped my fear of arranged marriage. I was now afraid that I might be eaten in a horrible culinary accident. Lucky for me, neither is likely to happen. Major General Karim has been selected for promotion and has moved up to the Division Headquarters, which I assume includes a larger kitchen staff. I am still hoping that his deputy, a very competent English speaking colonel, will take the brigade, but it appears they will be moving him elsewhere and bringing in a draft choice to be named later. So, the engagement is off for now.

It is probably far too early to make many accurate observations, so I will leave you with a few first impressions. The traffic in Baghdad is much less busy than I recall from two years ago, and the drivers far better trained. We used to fight our way from place to place, as Iraqis darted in and out of convoys. Now they go out of the way to pull over and wait for U.S. and Iraqi forces convoys to pass. At first look, the Iraqi National Police are more capable than the Iraqi Army was two years ago. Actually, I find myself pleasantly surprised by some of the things they are doing. They will never do things quite like we do, but they are performing well inside their own set of cultural norms that has more in common with *The Sopranos* than *The Band of Brothers*. However, the enemy situation is far more complex than it was two years ago. Getting your head around it is no small task. I do not think it is going to happen any time this week.

Figure 14: "Gary" the terp

Figure 15: Sarkis Vrej Arkesmousasia "Saki" at FOB Justice

Figure 16: Rafid Kareem Mohammed "Rafid" at FOB Prosperity

Figure 17: Lieutenant Colonel Green (left) and Dhafir Mohammed
Baker "Victor" (right)

Update #4: 5 February 2007— Raid

The moon was full, but the weather had become increasingly thick throughout the afternoon and evening. By 0100 in the morning, the wind was howling and the ominous clouds all but obscured the moon—perfect trick-or-treating weather. Fortunately, treats were on the agenda and as my HMMWV (vehicle) crested the rise, a convoy of National Police trucks lined up at the checkpoint exactly where they were supposed to be and right on time.

This would be my team's first real combat mission. We have done a variety of trips around Baghdad but in each instance we were deliberately trying to stay out of trouble. Tonight we were looking for it. The 5th Brigade had been tracking a group of improvised explosive device (IED) makers[3] for several months and we finally got the last piece of information we needed to go snatch them out of their beds. The National Police were excited. Jabba the Hut had not let them do raids in almost nine months, and the new commander was testing the waters. They worked up a good plan, so my team, along with one of

---

[3] This particular cell was a Shia faction cell belonging to the Jesh Al-Mahdi (JAM). They had been planting IEDs on a major east west crossroads in the Mansoor district, and had also been part of the ethnic cleansing of that particular neighborhood.

my subordinate teams would fight along with them. It was a great opportunity to get both teams some seasoning. I was the only U.S. member who had ever done a raid, so we would all earn our stripes together. No doubt, both groups were watching the other carefully.

We slowly rolled to the front of their column taking the opportunity to inspect them and count their vehicles. If push came to shove, I needed to know how many Iraqi trucks I had to bring home. Seventeen. Exactly what they had told me. More importantly, they had brought their "cracker box" (ambulance). They have just recently gotten their ambulances, and in typical Iraqi fashion, they are not inclined to actually use them. It is much more prestigious to have it than to actually use it. As we formulated the plan, I left little doubt that I expected it to be there. They had not argued, nor did they disappoint—another treat. Even more importantly, they were all wearing their helmets and body armor. This is no small accomplishment. I may have exaggerated a bit when I told them that my troops tended to shoot people running around an objective at night unless they had a Kevlar and body armor on to identify them, but they were not taking any chances. I bet it will not be as easy when the weather hits 125 degrees. We shall see.

I link up with the commander on the ground for a last minute update before execution. It is actually the deputy battalion commander as the commander was on leave. Lieutenant Colonel Abdula is a great big, tall Iraqi with square features. Iraqi commanders dress pretty much as they please. Abdul is sporting a knee length black leather jacket over his green battle dress uniform. His Kevlar helmet is firmly strapped to his head, an assault rifle trails from one hand, and the other waves the stub of a cigar. The lights are dim, and for a second I almost thought I had stepped onto the set of a WWII movie and was about to talk to Storm Trooper Shultz of the Waffen SS. I come back to reality just in time to make the correct hand gesture, and placed my right hand over my heart…. "aSalam alykum, saydee." We are the same rank, but I use the honorific sir, so he knows that I know he is in charge tonight. He flashes a grin around the embers of his cigar. "Alykum aSalam."

He has three young lieutenants lined up, each ready and eager to back-brief the two of us on the objectives they will hit. Damn, they look young! However, all three know their role tonight. Like lieutenants throughout the ages, they are excited and eager. I am impressed; these guys are much better than I remember from two years ago. Everything is in order so we give the signal to mount up. As we stalk back to my truck, Lieutenant Colonel Abdula gives a final shout to his subordinates. I glance at my terp and raised an eyebrow. "Sir, he told them they better not abuse anyone we detain." I smile, "So Rafid, you think he said that for show?" Rafid is a cynic so his answer surprised me a bit. "Sir, he speaks enough English that if he wanted you to hear it, he would have said it in your language." Interesting. Back into the night.

Minutes later we arrive in the target area. We take a creative route; one that we hope will avoid the lookouts who we know provide early warning when Coalition forces and Iraqi security forces enter the area. The neighborhood is pitch black. The power grid is off and the locals are not wealthy enough to run generators. The only movement on the streets is trash tumbling in the wind and a few mangy dogs that begin keeping pace with our trucks. They do not bark. Iraqis do not like dogs. These animals are not pets; they are scavengers. They will provide no early warning to those who fear and despise them. My teams spread out, able to watch each of the various Iraqi elements but still cover each other. So far, the execution is flawless, and by all observable measures, we have achieved surprise. The shurtas (police) dismount and stack on three separate target buildings. Two enter unopposed, the third finds the entrance locked and must force a breach.

"SHIT!" The radio nets come alive, even as our pupils begin to dilate. The jig is up, and someone has activated the power grid for the entire block. The neon lights of a neighborhood supermarket flare to life, and windows previously dark now spill light into the streets.

"Spartan, this is Spartan Six, keep calm and keep your eyes open for any new lights coming on." Telling folks to keep calm and keeping calm are two different things. We now knew that we were being watched. The only question left was if it was by anyone who had the muscle to do something about it. Seconds stretched out into minutes—still no movement. No additional lights. Nothing. Nothing was almost more unnerving than the gunfire everyone expected. The Iraqi radio crackled. One detainee in the first house—they were mounting up. The second house follows shortly after, with three more detainees (these turn out to be the criminals we are looking for). The final house takes a bit more time and nets four more suspects and some weapons. I glance at my watch. We are doing great. We collapse off the objective in good order. Leaving is always the worst part in my mind. I count seventeen Iraqi trucks. We rendezvous at the agreed upon location.

Lieutenant Colonel Abdula meets me on the ground. He looks worried. We exchange the ritual greetings and I tell him I thought it went very well. He is quick with an apology. He had told me it would take thirty minutes. It had taken forty-five. I had expected ninety. I clap him on the back. "The chai will taste just as good at 0215 as it would have at 0200." He agrees and drops the subject. We walk the line of his vehicles. I want to see the reactions of the shurta. They look proud and excited. They spend most of their time in very boring and dangerous checkpoint operations, usually on the defensive. Taking the offense is good for the soul. I count detainees. Eight who are all in one piece. Good.

I head back to my HMMWV. The same look of pride and excitement shows in my team's faces. I offer a quick prayer of thanks for an easy first excursion; there will certainly be harder days to come.

Figure 18: Joint 5-2NP and 5-2NPTT patrol

Update #5: 19 February 2007— Colonel Bahaa

Colonel Bahaa Noori Yassin Al Azawi and I converse beside my HMMWV while we watch his shurta conduct an impromptu checkpoint. His personal security detachment has dispersed around the park where we wait for a link up with a Ministry of Interior press secretary and camera crews. My team provides overwatch. As part of the surge, the brigade moved to a new compound and was assigned a new area of operations.

Colonel Bahaa had been the deputy commander of the 5th Brigade and has finally been officially assigned as the commander. To date, he is exactly what I had hoped for in a counterpart. About ten years my senior, he flew MIG-21s as a young officer and eventually transferred to air defense when the Iraqi Air Force ceased to exist in 1991. Since the fall of Saddam, he has served in the National Police. A Sunni in a predominantly Shia organization, he has survived by being competent but is well behind his peers in rank because he has avoided much of the nepotism. He has no end of energy, personal courage, or good humor. He reminds me a bit of a ferret, always happy and always looking for something new to do. I should note that he spent two years studying in England as a young officer. He speaks and reads English fluently, making my job significantly easier.

Our vehicles are parked along a well-trafficked road near the International Zone. It runs the length of a park, which is full of workers doing a variety of tasks. I watch a small crew mix cement and pour it around wire frames, creating fake log arches, benches and tables. A gardener makes a credible attempt at a lawn, and a few flowers augment what are largely rock gardens. I am not surprised to see that kind of work so close to the heart of the government. However, I have seen it in multiple neighborhoods throughout the areas we have traveled. There is a section along the river in the north that is undertaking a massive new sidewalk project using European style bricks in intricate patterns. Maybe spring makes folks want to clean up. The city is bipolar in its sanitation with some areas making huge strides to keep clean while others dump trash in the streets as fast as they can create it.

The press finally shows up, and we pile them into the National Police vehicles and head north. Traffic is initially heavy, but quickly thins as we approach the south end of Haifa Street. In the distance, the modern high rises of Haifa look untouched by war, and indeed the ones at the south end largely are. The bright colors and palm trees remind me of the main tourist street in Honolulu. Distance is a great deceiver, and as we get closer, it becomes clear that we are in no tropical paradise. As we weave through our first checkpoint and the streets become more deserted, signs of war become more evident. We turn at the first corner and find ourselves transported to Mogadishu. We weave down around a turn and open into a city square along the bank of the Tigris that is complete with a Soviet style statue of a dead Iraqi general and a wide, deserted bridge. This was like a strange Universal Studios tour. In less than a mile, I had gone from the set of *Baywatch*, to *Blackhawk Down*, to *Enemy at the Gates*.

Colonel Bahaa's men secure the square. Residents slowly emerge from ravaged storefronts and homes. We dismount and the press conference begins. I stay at the fringes, letting Bahaa and the Ministry spokesperson do their thing. A small crowd forms, a phenomenon sparked by cameras the world over. The group moves out onto the bridge for a better shot. Shit. As if the sniper threat was not bad enough amongst the high-rise buildings, let us stroll out onto the bridge! Breathe in ... step off. The questions continue. I put my back against a pillar and watch. After several minutes, I pick my name out the babble of Arabic. This is not my day. Colonel Bahaa's head pops up out of the huddle and scans quickly for me. He waves me over. I take my goggles off, remembering that tip from repeated public affairs classes. Sadly, forty hours of Arabic training flush from my brain faster than a commode at an Ex-Lax festival. Mercifully, the reporter spoke English and asked a few easy questions. A ruckus that starts behind me puts me out of my misery. I am not sure how it started, but one of Colonel Bahaa's bodyguards began singing, causing the others to quickly cluster up into a traditional display of Arab military might—the AK-47 dance. Sweet! As if the danger of snipers was not enough, now my own Iraqis are about ready to fire into the air and bring down a light drizzle of lead. Thankfully, they are too busy smiling for the camera to pull the trigger. I motion to my two dismounted teammates and start moving Bahaa back to the trucks. His personal security detachment remembers their duty and scramble to get back in place.

Back in the square, we head off for the real purpose of the trip. Down a side street even more decrepit than the last, a maternity hospital closed, apparently two years ago. I have no idea how true that is, but as we enter, it would not surprise me. One of our subordinate Iraqi infantry battalions, the 1-1-6th IA[4], cleared the building out the day before, displacing squatters. Bahaa's men now take up residence on the ground floor to secure it. As we begin the tour, guards clear ahead of us while the press busily film and take pictures. The place is a disaster, but has potential. We climb to the second floor and head to another wing. Up another flight, past elevators that do not work— sigh—into another stairwell and up again. Body armor begins taking a

---

[4]   One of the significant changes brought about as part of "the Surge" strategy was integrating the chains of command of Iraqi Army (which worked for the Minister of Defense) and the National Police (which worked for the Minister of the Interior) into one unified structure. This was not an easy process and generated significant friction in the spring of 2007. In the case of the 5th Brigade, Colonel Bahaa did not have direct command of any of his three organic National Police Battalions. They were working in other districts. Instead he had been given operational control of the 1-1-6 BN Iraqi Army, the 3-5-6BN Iraqi Army, and the National Police Quick Reaction Force Battalion. Later in the year, that task organization would change several times, and eventually the Brigade found itself all back in the same district.

toll on the calves. We arrive at the top floor, the ninth, and I pause to wipe my brow and catch a breath. Lieutenant Colonel Ali, one of my Iraqi operations officers, grins at me from across the room.

Several weeks ago when we first met, he was outside the headquarters wearing a running suit and a high-speed pair of running shoes. Now, 1970's sports attire is the style here, so that was not unusual, but he actually looked like he might be getting ready to exercise. He informed me that he had been a tri-athlete in his younger days and still liked to run. He challenged me to a race. I will give those of you who know me well a few minutes to recover from the fit of laughter you are suffering from. Okay, let us continue. I smile and tell him that I will have to do a bit of training. Then I suggest it may be more fun to have my team play them in soccer some day. Pleasantries exchanged, we went about our business. Weeks later and nine floors higher he pushes through the crowded room and in broken English declares "Score, me one, you zero." We laugh. He is wearing no body armor. I ask if he wants to wear mine back down. He smiles, "No, then it would be tied one to one!"

The party breaks up. The mob descends and begins the trip back to civilization. We hope we can make this place safe enough to reopen. It will not be easy. The neighborhood has suffered terribly. Over the last few days, we found several caches of weapons and arrested a variety of terrorists, insurgents and criminals-all flavors of unspeakable evil. The more we patrol, and the longer our troops remain in the neighborhoods, the more information we get. Every day more and more folks are willing to venture into the streets and more shops open. After just a week, the difference is noticeable. We expect to more than double the size of our force in the next thirty days. Right now, we have about ten uniformed Iraqis in the street for every American. The surge will give us more of both and, hopefully, tip the scales in our favor if only in the small area that we are responsible for. It is far from rosy. There are some unspeakable things happening, sometimes by those arguably on our side. One step at a time.

Necessary is not always easy.

Figure 19: Leka Maternity Hospital in the left foreground with the Holland high rise appartments on Haifa Street behind

Update #6: 4 March 07—The Orphanage

My driver took a hard turn off a traffic circle and into the narrow road that leads to my brigade's barracks. To one side is an old dried up creek bed that now looks much more like a river of trash than anything resembling water. When the Police Brigade I advise first moved into its newly renovated barracks almost a month ago, the river served mostly as a dumping ground. Times they are a changing, and as the unit secured the neighborhood and began monitoring who comes and goes, the ecology of the riverbed has changed. Within a week, small children began swimming in the stream of filth. Most of the waste is paper or plastic, anything organic has long since been devoured by the river's other native life form—the wild dog.

By the second week, the children had cleared out two soccer fields, absolutely spotless islands of dirt, around which the rubbish continues to flow. Always looking for creative ways to win the war, my guys have decided that the Prime Minister should declare the entire city a soccer inclusion zone, and we could solve the refuse problem overnight. If it works, I am running for governor of New Jersey. By week three, a pair of real soccer goals adorned the larger of the islands, and teams of young adults were playing organized games several nights a week with jerseys and referees. At first, it was just the teams. By the end of the week, there were fans. Most do not pay much attention as we drive

41

by. The little kids do. We toss candy on random days to keep them guessing. It is our own little Pavlov's dog experiment.

When we made the turn yesterday, there were many fans…maybe four hundred. Both teams were wearing jerseys we had not seen before. We have yet to figure out who is the home team. I think it is the yellow shirts. Today was red vs. black. As my trail truck made the turn, red scored on black. The moment my lead truck had been waiting for had finally arrived! Staff Sergeant Pettus, the driver, picked up his microphone (we have loudspeakers so we can broadcast) and yelled "GOOOOOAAAAAL," in true European fashion. Red found it as amusing as we did. Black did not. We assume black are the insurgents.

Several hours later, we pass the Baghdad Zoo. To call it a zoo may be a bit generous, as there have not been animals in it since we saw the lions running the streets on CNN several years ago. However, the park still exists, but it is closed to the public. For the last several weeks, our brigade has secured the perimeter. It is a sunny weekend afternoon, and earlier in the day, Colonel Bahaa decided to open the park. When we drove by in the morning a few cars had ventured in, and small groups of folks meandered on the paths around artificial lakes. By afternoon, cars half filled the parking lot. Pedestrians lined up to be searched before entering. A grandmother smiled as she takes two little ones in. Both are young enough that it must have been their first visit.

Figure 20: Entrance to the Baghdad Zoo

Many years ago, I remember watching a documentary on orphanages in Czechoslovakia or Romania. It talked about the horrible neglect and long term effects on the children when taken from their mothers at birth and essentially denied any real human contact for the first formative years of their life. Many of those children found themselves subsequently adopted by American families and met with various levels of success or failure.

As my team embraces our new area of responsibility, I cannot help but feel like part of a family that has just adopted a little Czech orphan. For whatever reason, the area has been largely untouched in a persistent way by either U.S. or Iraqi forces. They have come in to feed and change it, but then left it in the crib to cry. The signs of neglect are evident and violent tantrums are not at all uncommon. As of February's new security plan enabled by the surge, the baby is in a new home, one that has both a father and a mother.

This story has gone largely untold. Sadly, the media is so completely uneducated in politics and war that they have no idea what to report even if it is clearly in front of them. They have almost solely focused on the adopting father. Story after story documents the increase in U.S. troop levels, and they have completely missed all the other far more important things that the change in strategy is built upon. There is a mother involved in all of this—the Iraqi security forces. What is largely unexplained is that there has been a surge within Iraq as well. Units from all over Iraq have repositioned into Baghdad. It probably goes unnoticed because deploying an American unit is not that big a deal. Not so for an average Iraqi unit.

Let us start with a quick look at the nature of the Iraqi recruiting system, one that arguably produces a force that is even more "voluntary" than our own. I do not know the origin of the decision, but when Iraqi's enlist, they do not sign up for a standard tour as we do. They join, serve, and if they do not like it, they leave, usually by just going AWOL (absent without leave) and never returning. Because there is no punishment for desertion, there is really no incentive to keep them on the job. If life presents a better opportunity or if the dangers become too great, they walk away. Moreover, they tend to join units based in geographical areas or based on who the commanders are. You cannot underestimate the power of nepotism. When the Iraqi government decides to pick up a unit, move it across the country and employ it somewhere far from home, it is a big deal and has the potential to break the unit.

Consider a thirty-year-old Iraqi male from a town in northern Iraq with a family that depends on him. If he deploys to Baghdad for several months, how does he provide for them? He is paid in cash, and there is no banking system to speak of (that is a cultural thing ... we did not destroy it). He cannot wire the money home, so he has to take it home on leave. When he does so, he risks his safety getting there and back, and may spend a significant chunk of his monthly pay just to get home and return. You cannot discount the anxiety of leaving your family unsecured in a country where ethnic hatred is creating all sorts of random violence. What keeps him in the service then? It is hard to say, but many are taking serious risks to serve. It may seem like the Iraqis are not meeting "benchmarks" at the aggregate level, but life is very rarely about aggregates.

So he sticks it out, and tries to do the right thing. His unit gets to Baghdad. Where do we put them? Well if it is a Kurdish unit, and many are, wherever they go may cause a stir. The Kurdish population here is relatively small, which may be a part of the problem, but I digress. The poor soldier may not even speak Arabic. So now he is patrolling the streets of a strange city, with people he cannot talk to, and who might just hate him for being different. Wow, sounds like a U.S. soldier—but he is an Iraqi! He needs interpreters just to talk to other elements in his own army. With the possible exception of a few units from Puerto Rico, at least all the U.S. forces can speak to each other. Imagine how hard reconstructing the south after the Civil War would have been if troops from New York and Massachusetts spoke a different language. At any rate, this is what the Iraqi Armed Forces have done. It is a big step forward. Moreover, they have made a second huge step by reorganizing their command structure. Previously, the Iraqi Army, Iraqi National Police, Iraqi Police, Iraqi Traffic Police, and River Patrol, etc ... all worked for their own chains of command, and rarely if ever interacted. Not only that, but also most of them had open contempt for the other and often warred against each other. The new plan has forced each district to merge their leadership and National Policemen find themselves both commanding and commanded by the Iraqi Army in integrated chains of command. I cannot underestimate the importance of this overlooked change. Nor am I going to tell you that the new mom is happy about it. Sometimes she is confused ... not sure if she should spank the child or put him in time out. She does not always get it right. As in most things, it is largely a matter of the people involved. However, in the areas where it is working, we are seeing dramatic results.

A couple other relatives in the "surge" family are helping to raise the child. The media has noticed the training teams; the job my team is doing. We are much like grandparents. We get a completely different look at mother and father, as well as the child. In a perfect world, we can help keep the child from playing mother off against father and vice versa. In homes where mother and father are consistent with the baby, things are going well.

I do not know if this poor Czech baby can be saved. I do know it is going to take mother, father, and grandparents to do it. We are going to have to be able to pick the child up early and often.

Update #7: 11 March 2007—The Zoo

I sat in Colonel Bahaa's office drinking chai. We drink lots of chai. His office is typical, a desk at one end that is adorned with a standard western style collection of name placards, blotters, phones, and memorabilia. It is rarely used. The work happens in the couches that line the walls. A collection of one, two, and three person overstuffed low-slung couches, all brand new, line two walls. He has spent a good chunk of cash on them I am sure. The fourth wall is the home of the obligatory TV. Depending on the time of day, it alternates between the news and the ever-popular Arabic or Indian music videos. I am far more in tune with Bollywood than Hollywood these days. A set of three low tables round out the room; they are in constant motion around the room as guests come and go and are served various meals. I average at least one meal here a day. I try to bring desserts or snacks with me when I can. I hate that they are paying out of pocket to feed me. They hate it when they do not have the opportunity to play host.

Every important Iraqi has what the Americans refer to as the "chai guy." The chai guy is on the unit's books, and is usually a close relative or friend. They never wear a uniform; or rather, the uniform is typically a 1970's sweat suit usually with a misspelled logo. While they do not look the part, they are essentially a British butler. They slide in and out of meetings, arranging tables, pouring chai, adding and subtracting chairs in a never-ending dance. Colonel Bahaa has two chai guys, Imod and Haydr. Both are in their mid-thirties. Given their responsibilities to keep the food and drink flowing, it is not surprising that both are a bit heavy. To American eyes, the job would seem demeaning, but they are both proud of what they do and enjoy a certain place in the hierarchy. Imod is the leader of the two and does the shopping. Haydr is a bit slow, but exceptionally diligent. In many ways, they are like Colonel Bahaa's children.

On the slow days, Colonel Bahaa will joke with them. He plays a game with Haydr, where he summons him very close like he is going to give him some private instruction. Haydr will lean in to receive a whisper, and Colonel Bahaa will poke him quickly in the gut and shout "Hiya!" Without fail, Haydr will jump straight to the ceiling much to the amusement of all present. The game repeats several times, with Haydr jumping out of his skin even though he knows what is coming. Eventually Colonel Bahaa rewards him with the actual instructions and he runs back out to happily perform his chores.

Figure 21: Colonel Bahaa enjoying a Hookah

The radio crackles "Ares Six, this is Ares one-three ... you have got to come see this!" (We had to change our radio call sign when we moved to our new area ... too many Spartans running around. However, we had already painted Greek helmets on everything so we kept with the theme.)

"One-three, Six, what do I need to see?"

"Sir, just step outside."

I wander out the front gate of the headquarters to watch a squad of shurta chasing a sheep around the compound. It was very clear that none of them had any Texan in them. This rodeo was going nowhere fast. After several laps around the yard, the terrified sheep fled out into the barracks area and into the resting place of the local pack of wild dogs. More scared of this new foe than the bumbling shurta, the sheep doubled back and found itself caught. It was mid-afternoon, so I figured this was dinner waiting to happen. Normally there are one or two sheep in the compound awaiting their fate. Usually the shepherd who raises them marks them with red or green spray paint to identify his flock. We joke that it is a born on freshness date. Eat the red one by mid month and the blue one by month's end.

The victorious shurta deliver the now passive sheep to Imod, who lays it out on the front steps of the HQ and effortlessly slits its neck allowing the blood to pool on the stone tiles. What he did next surprised me. He dipped his hand in the blood and then placed it on the window of the front door leaving a perfect handprint. I glanced at Colonel Bahaa and raised an eyebrow.

Colonel Bahaa talks in a low voice, the way he does when he is teaching me something. "You see, this morning I told you that Lieutenant Mahmoud had been injured." Lieutenant Mahmoud is the leader of Colonel Bahaa's personal security guard. His vehicle had been hit by an IED that morning, and he had received a shrapnel wound to the leg. He will be fine, but only because Colonel Bahaa paid out of his pocket to send him to a private hospital. "It is a bad omen that he was wounded, so they are sacrificing a sheep so that its blood will replace human blood, and we will not be attacked again." He paused. "They are superstitious." Note to self: buy stock in sheep.

The next day we conduct a mission to serve warrants in one of our more troublesome neighborhoods. It goes without a hitch, and we gather up another crop of evil doers. Haydr drives out to the objective to deliver chai while we process the detainees. He grins from ear to ear. Colonel Bahaa looks at his watch; we are done several hours earlier than we had planned. He grins at me the way he does when he is ready to spring something unexpected on me. "Let's go to the zoo!"

"The zoo Saydee?"

"Naam, the zoo. We are early and we have all our troops. We will search it and make sure it is safe. And see how it has been doing now that it has been open for a week."

"Ok, the zoo it is. Lead on."

We pull into the front gates with about two hundred soldiers. They do not make us pay the 25 cents to get in. He barks orders quickly, and the shurta fan out in small squads and begin searching the grounds. Bahaa and I make our way with our guards to the park administration building. What we find actually surprises me. While the zoo has not been open for ages, the staff has been busy and maintains a small collection of animals. I was under the misconception that there were not any. We get the VIP tour.

The facilities are all 1970's era amusement park style, all reasonably well maintained, even if the bright colored paint schemes have faded to pastel in the harsh summer sun. The grounds are relatively free of trash, and gardeners fill nearly every flowerbed in an effort to get the zoo up to snuff. We cross over the train tracks. The three-car train is not yet running, but they are hopeful to have it running in a week or two.

We enter the exhibit area, past the peacocks, vulture, and falcon, to the zoo's main attraction—a pride of four gorgeous female lions. They are well cared for and have a great deal of space. Who would have guessed? In the next space are two huge cheetahs. The keeper invites me to go in and pet them. I figure that 70 pounds of body armor should be able to stop the worst of a cheetah attack. I am game, but the zoo administrator puts the kibosh on the invitation. We pass a pair of badgers, a trio of porcupine and a huge wild boar. Colonel Bahaa proudly names them all off as we go. When we get to the boar he looks at me, winks, and proclaims "Bacon!"

We arrive at the camel cage. A single large frothy mouthed beast lounges lazily against the cage. The shurta all want pictures next to the camel for some inexplicable reason as it is the one animal they have all almost certainly seen before. Several of the personal security detachment line up while I pull a camera out. All of a sudden from the ass end of the camel, a rumbling begins that boils up out of its gut, through its stomach, building momentum up the long neck and finally exploding from flapping lips in the largest and most foul smelling burp imaginable. I look to the zookeeper thinking, "What are you feeding that thing?" The shurta decide pictures are not so important.

We move on to the monkey yard. About six different species of monkey inhabit the area. One particularly foul tempered monkey draws our attention. One of the shurta squats down in front of the cage and takes the cigarette out of his mouth to start talking monkey talk. The chimp takes offense at whatever comment was made and with lightning fast reflexes, snatches the lit cigarette from his hand and proceeds to swallow it whole. My concern for the feeding program was rising exponentially.

We visit the small aquarium. Sadly, they have no fish. I cannot imagine it would take much of an investment to fix this. We have about finished the tour. Unfortunately, only about twenty-five percent of the exhibit space has occupants. Nevertheless, as we have traveled, families and couples are clearly delighted to be here. They are strangely relaxed in spite of the heavy military presence we are imposing on them. By now, Colonel Bahaa's men have finished the search and have been released to meander around the zoo. The bodyguards remain vigilant, but the rest begin to mix with the civilians. One group received an invitation to a picnic, by cousins they happen upon. Others head to the snack stands for gyros or kabobs. Colonel Bahaa shells out cash and loads his guards up with sodas and ice cream.

We stroll out past the lake. About ten couples float lazily in small paddleboats. Three shurta race around the pond in a small blue one. I am sure it is only built for two. They see their commander, and with the international look of "Oh crap, there is the boss," they sheepishly cry out "Saydee! We are looking for insurgents hiding in the pond." They get the laughter they hoped for and proceed to paddle for shore without a reprimand.

All around the pond, young couples sit on park benches, heads held close talking about whatever young lovers talk about. I have to wonder what plans and dreams they dare hatch amidst all this uncertainty. Colonel Bahaa is a bit of a romantic. He proclaims, "I am proud to see all the young lovers in the park. It makes me happy." I cannot help but think back to my childhood when every car seemed to have a "Virginia is for Lovers" bumper sticker. I tell Colonel Bahaa that we could make a fortune selling "Baghdad Zoo is for Lovers" bumper stickers. We decide that this is what we will do when we retire.

We head home. It has been a strange twenty-four hours.

Update #8: 23 March 2007—Trust

I vaguely remember one of my literature teachers telling me that good writing should serve to both educate and delight. That seems like good advice, and I try to make sure I do both in these updates, especially as the audience grows. I never really know what I am going to write about next. So much of what we do is classified. It is not possible just to describe things as they happen. To be honest, many of the stories would start sounding the same. Therefore, I usually wait for some sort of inspiration that ties a few images or tales together. I got that today when I came back from a particularly successful district area council meeting where we are really beginning to gain some traction.

I opened up my computer and scanned the headlines from the major wireless services. Once again, my faith in the American press's ability to use responsibly the freedom of speech a generation is fighting to defend was shattered. "Poll shows Iraqis don't trust Americans!" "Only 19% of Iraqis trust Americans:" blah, blah, blah ... drivel, drivel, poppycock. Story after story reciting some poll without ever explaining any of the methods used to take the poll, or when they took it. No accountability whatsoever. I would bet this month's pay that the poll is at least thirty days old. I bet the pollsters have enjoyed about four or five weekends and a couple of national holidays sitting on all that useful data. Meanwhile twenty-year-old American and Iraqi patriots put their lives on the line without break to actually fix the problems about which the brave pollsters cannot even articulate decent questions.

I would love to know how they collected that data. I bet it was not door-to-door. If it were, I would probably have seen the soldiers tasked to guard them. By telephone? I wonder what percentage of folks have a cell phone and where they are located regionally. Even without my rocket science degree I can pretty well determine that the telephone will not get you an even representation in Iraq. Mail? Sorry friends, Cliff does not get off his barstool at *Cheers* to deliver mail to Haifa Street … even in good weather.

I wonder about the questions not asked in the poll. Did they ask what percentage of Iraqis trust Iraqis? Would it be higher or lower than the 19% level afforded to Americans? Next month's paycheck says that it is less. I am not an expert on Arab culture by any means, but I am certain of this. Arabs do not trust anyone unless they have looked them in the eye, eaten with them and included them in their circle of friends. Trust builds over time and is not given easily. They do not do any business on the first meeting, or the second, or often the third. They will judge you and judge you again until they find you worthy. Then, when they do finally start calling you friend, you will be in the family and they will do anything for you. The default answer to any poll question asked about trust is going to be "no."

Here are some examples of Iraqis I have met. You judge if they trust us.

Several weeks ago we conducted a cordon and search operation[5] to serve warrants on a list of about sixty individuals. We rounded up about forty. Iraqi names are often very similar, and sometimes you do not get the right people. In this particular search, the Iraqis detained a

---

[5] A Cordon and Search Operation generally consists of a significant area of terrain being surrounded by a sizable force of troops to prevent anyone from entering or leaving. A second group of troops then methodically searches everything inside the cordon, looking for contraband, caches, or suspect individuals. Such operations had mixed results. Sometimes they uncovered previously unknown problems. Sometimes, they generated ill will with the population and generated entirely new problems. The cordon and search operations conducted by the 5th Brigade in February and March of 2007 would provide examples of both. They did however allow Brigadier General Bahaa to force all the units under his new command to start working together.

guy with an Egyptian accent. For a variety of good reasons, the Iraqis assume that non-Iraqis are here as foreign fighters. This particular gentleman was relatively old, probably in his sixties, so I was a bit skeptical. While we were processing all the detainees, he began faking seizures. My medic examines everyone we detain at the point of capture and every few days afterwords at the detainee facility to make certain there is no abuse. He was convinced that the old codger was faking. It is common. Almost everyone ever pulled from their home has a bottle of pills for some life threatening illness that they have to go back to get. At any rate, this old man went through the process, and after a few days, the Iraqis determined that he had no information of value and we escorted him back to his neighborhood. Weeks later, Colonel Bahaa and I conducted a foot patrol through that neighborhood talking to residents. When we arrived at the bottom of the alleyway, we heard a ruckus and the Egyptian broke through the crowd and greeted both Colonel Bahaa and I as if we were long lost friends. My medic was with us and got a warm hug and thanks for the placebos he gave the man for his seizures. (I am sure the Motrin helped him feel better, but had little effect on his seizures) He invited us down to his market stall and insisted that we eat fruit with him. I am confident that he trusts Colonel Bahaa and me. He knows we treated him fairly, and so do the folks in his little community.

We went into a school around the corner—an elementary school for boys. We sat with the male schoolmaster and three female teachers. They were actually excited to talk with us, and contrary to many of the myths, the women engaged us openly. They are happy to be back to work after months of being too terrified to open the schools. I asked how many of the kids are actually back at school. They tell me that about half are back; the remaining parents are waiting to see if the next month is as good as the last. I asked why they feel safer now ... why they think the violence is down? The response is that they have Iraqi units permanently assigned to the checkpoints in the neighborhoods, and they see Americans working with them.

We negotiated a busy traffic circle the other day. An Iraqi motorcycle cop was in hot pursuit of a man on a moped and they both careened into the traffic circle to my right rear. A car saw us and stopped abruptly. The moped slipped past, but the motorcycle clipped the car sending the patrol officer flying off the bike. All I saw was a while helmet fly past my window! That was strange enough that I ordered a halt. My trail vehicle saw what happened, so we helped clear the scene and my doc and terps went to work. It did not take long for the Iraqi ambulance to arrive on the scene, but the common response from the Iraqi police who arrived to help their comrade was "Thanks, we are glad you got to see him first."

Today we drove through a busy market. As I admired a narrow alley overflowing with fruit stands and wished I had my camera to capture the colors, I watched a middle-aged man collapse for no reason. We stopped. Doc got to work and quickly assessed that he had passed out due to dehydration. An old man helped keep the crowd away from us and as we left, he told us that he is glad that we stopped when we did not have to. He wished us safe travels and was glad we are finally back in the area to help. No pollster had to coerce that response from him. He could have easily stayed in the crowd and said nothing.

About an hour before, a group that wanted to tell us something stopped us. It was in an area we have visited often (near the Egyptian man). The kids all recognize us. Candy has that effect. They know several of us by name and ask us to stop. We find a safe spot and pull over. The kids bring over a few young adults who are asking about their brother. They are concerned because a National Police unit came and took him yesterday, obviously, because he was a Sunni and most police are Shia. I start asking questions. "What did the vehicle look like? How many trucks were in the patrol? What did the uniforms look like? What time of day?" The answers all match my suspicions. I tell them "The only guy the National Police arrested yesterday in this neighborhood was selling fuel."

"Yes, that's him!" They cried.

"Oh really, and he was selling fuel on the side of the road?"

"Yes, that is what he does."

"You know that the Prime Minister has made selling black market fuel illegal?"

"Well, yes."

"Did you know that the commander who arrested him is Sunni?"

"No."

"So is it possible that they arrested him because he was breaking the law and not because he is Sunni?"

Pause … The adults who have gathered all glance at each other.

Grudgingly, "Yes. But is he OK?"

"Yes, we saw him this morning. We check the detainees every day."

"Good, we understand that he was caught doing illegal things, we just don't want him killed. If you are checking then we know they will not kill him. We trust the Americans, but not the police."

"You know that I don't get to go home till you start trusting them more than you trust me?"

They laugh.

"I am really looking forward to going home!"

One of the first people the National Police detained when we got here was a very odd Taliban looking guy. He had the full out-of-control beard and traditional Arab dress. That is actually very unusual in Baghdad. He had been casing one of the checkpoints and the police noticed his suspicious behavior and detained him. He was so nasty and dirty that he had fungus growing on him. When they brought him in for questioning, we were just arriving at the headquarters. They had him kneeling on the ground in the intelligence officer's office asking him some questions. The intelligence officer had told us before we went in that he was sure the detainee was Al Qaeda and had had some brainwashing. The prisoner wore a blindfolded, so did not see the Americans enter the room. We listened to the questioning. After several minutes, one of my team members asked a question. The sound of an American voice hit him like a brick. He collapsed to the floor and began reciting the Koran repeatedly, refusing to come out of the trance. He trusted Americans too. He knew his chance for martyrdom was over.

We win trust one person at a time. It requires looking them in the eye and convincing them that you are just like them. It requires courage. It requires a commitment to stay the course. It requires consistent ethical behavior. Over time acquaintances become neighbors, neighbors become friends and friends become brothers. Candy may win the kids, but consistency wins the adults. It is too bad that there is no magic pill to cure the attention deficit disorder of a nation. Ours could use one.

Update #9: 29 March 2007— Patrol

The noise of the engine rumbles steadily as we creep along. In spite of the decibels constantly bombarding the senses, the night seems quiet. The headset helps muffle some of the noise. I suppose the near total darkness tricks the ears and brain into assuming it is quiet. We have been patrolling for several hours, rolling at a slow and deliberate pace through each of the varied neighborhoods in our sector. It is small relative to other sectors, but has more diversity than most. From the richest to poorest, oldest to newest, the area provides a wide range of possibilities and pitfalls.

Our patrol started in the wealthy neighborhoods. The occasional streetlight and a fluorescent business sign light large homes, large even by our standards. The trash is mostly policed, and the sewage is under control. In many of the upstairs rooms you can see the obvious flicker of a TV set piping in some unknown show from a rooftop satellite. Curfew has been in effect for several hours and nothing moves in the streets, not even the expected pack of dogs or a stray cat. There is not enough trash to support them here, not when there is much better scrounging elsewhere.

We drive elsewhere. Clusters of high-rise apartment complexes house an untold number of residents. Close to the Green Zone, this area has had continuous occupants and infrequent violence. It too is largely lit. Powered more often than not by generators tied to apartment buildings rather than the city power grid, life is reasonably normal here day and night. However, nothing moves outside.

Back north to Haifa Street, to the area that reminds me of a movie studio lot. New shows film there during the day. Medical dramas replace war flicks. Last week our partnered U.S. unit did a medical assistance visit, setting up a temporary clinic in a school in the heart of the previously abandoned area. Residents have slowly begun trickling back to the apartments. Word spread quickly and the sick and needy came for care. The children swarmed about in packs. Colonel Bahaa made a statement for the cameras. I stood in the schoolyard surrounded by high rises. The face of this once thriving area is pockmarked by bullet and shell. The walls above the windows are stained by smoke and flames long since extinguished like the eyes of a crying woman whose mascara runs uncontrollably. Two months ago no one dared live above the bottom few floors. Everyone we talked to told stories of gunmen roving the upper stories at night randomly killing anyone who ventured out in the open. Today I watched a young woman on the eighth floor lower a rope to the ground and drag her belongings up to the balcony. I looked around and found two other families doing the same in adjacent buildings. The elevators are all broken.

The activity we saw during the day last week is not at all apparent on this night. Security forces patrol the streets, as do the dogs. There is much better rubbish here to sustain them. By and large, there is no power. However, the occasional window betrays a flicker. Small generators bring hope to rooms with windows heavily curtained to avoid waste or drawing attention. We continue on to the very poorest and oldest area in the shadows of the modern apartments.

The streets begin to narrow and twist. The houses grow increasingly smaller. We know they contain dozens packed in each tiny space. The streets here are flooded with children during the day. I joke with Colonel Bahaa that he has yet to take me to see the child factory that produces all these kids. He jokes that the child factory will go out of business if we can get the lights fixed and give the employees something else to do at night. Electricity is the single most frustrating problem we face. We make a turn at the bottom of the street and pass our problem.

An electrical substation huddles in the shadows. A dark lifeless corpse mounted on the wall of a cemetery, another unlikely victim of the war. About six months ago the oil-cooling tank on the substation sustained damage in the crossfire of some sectarian shootout. The oil bled out within minutes, leaving a sickly pool that still marks the death. Without oil, the substation overheated and blew in a shower of sparks. The neighborhood has been plunged into an era of darkness ever since. The corpse lay decomposing on the cemetery wall largely unnoticed. Now, six months later, we have the forces to do something about it, but progress is painfully slow in the eyes of the locals.

The houses here are pitch black, and have been for almost six hours since the sun went down. A crescent moon dimly lights the main streets, but the moon cannot penetrate the warren of slums where windows are rare. It will be another several hours before the sun entices the populace back out into the street. I cannot help but wonder what they tell their children in the darkest hours. How do they give comfort when the nightmares come? How do they help the little ones overcome the fear? How do they overcome it themselves? What do they think when the sounds of our vehicles pass? Are we guardian angels? Are we death squads sent by a militia to kill them? Are we going to raid their home and snatch a loved one away? In another place and another time I would expect to see lambs' blood lining the doorposts and lintels, biding the angel of death to pass over the house just one more night.

We drive on. Death will not visit tonight, or at least not that we observe. At the turn of the year, this area was reporting thirty murders a day. Daylight would find corpses arrayed on either side of the road marking the boundary between Sunni and Shia neighborhoods. Bodies were deliberately dragged from the scene of the crime and purposefully staged; each side striving to instill fear in the hearts and minds of the other. January saw over six hundred slaughtered. We are down now to a handful a week. Breaking the cycle of violence has been easier than we expected. How do you wipe that experience from the minds of the locals? How do they learn to forgive and forget? Something has to replace that fear. We hope we can start with light, resurrecting the metallic corpse tacked on the cemetery wall.

Several days later we patrol by day. We stop at the Soviet style statue down by the bridge. We have been back here several times since that first nervous press conference. Tradition lets soldiers who are reenlisting pick where they want to have it done. Staff Sergeant Ethington just signed on for another six years, great news for our Army. He decided he wanted to reenlist at that statue. I bring Colonel Bahaa down there with us to take part in the ceremony. Partly to educate him on how our process works, but also so he could hear the words of the oath that our soldiers take. He understands them and lives by very similar ideals. I want him to see that we work to instill those values in every soldier. He is pleased to participate; he knows it is important to Doc. We bring an American flag, but do not unfurl it. Doc holds it as he reaffirms his oath and we pose for photos. The shurta are curious. We take the opportunity to walk the street.

Figure 22: DOC's reenlistment at Adnon Statue. COL Bahaa, Staff Sergeant Ethington, and Lieutenant Colonel Green

We no longer shuffle through piles of trash. It is not clean by our standards, but sparkles in comparison to just a few weeks before. Much like visiting New York City before and after Rudy Giuliani's tenure as mayor. The difference is striking. We visit a newly opened café on the corner. The owner proudly proclaims that it is the oldest café in the district, which would make it one of the oldest in Baghdad. The expansive room looks larger than it really is due to an abnormally high ceiling and large columns that line the two open walls that face the corner of the street. The inside, painted what was once warm mustard, is now stained by smoke. At the back of the room is an open fireplace lined with white porcelain tiles. Old men drink chai and play dominoes at low tables. They grin toothless grins and exchange warm greetings as we enter. I could make a fortune turning this place into a Mexican cantina. Note to self: find mustard color paint.

On the way back home, the radio crackles. My terp translates quickly. Colonel Bahaa has stopped the convoy, but we are not getting out. That is a bit unusual. Not the stopping part, he is always stopping to correct one of his security forces, to talk to locals, or to investigate something that looks out of place. Therefore, it is very odd that he would stop but not dismount. Instead, one of his guys jumps out and darts into a local bakery. He comes out a few minutes later with box in hand. The radio crackles again "Ok, we can go." We do. We eat a late lunch. Sometimes it is just Colonel Bahaa and me. Sometimes the whole team eats. Often it is a mix. Today, it is just the Colonel and my two majors. We eat back in his private room, not out in his office. We had not done that before. The conversation is light. The chai guys keep us well cared for.

Colonel Bahaa loves desserts. He has been telling me about one of his favorites, which has an Arabic name I cannot remember that translates into "from the sky." I have no idea what ingredients are in "from the sky", and neither do they. The bakers keep it a guarded secret apparently. Served on a tray of flour, "from the sky" comes in small Oreo size globs. Sticky on the inside, the flour makes it possible to hold. It is not dough, nor is it taffy. Somehow, it is both, and contains nuts, probably pistachio. I love it, partly because I cannot figure out what it is. It is kind of like what you get if you knead a marshmallow for a few minutes, but not that sweet.

When we have eaten all we can eat, Colonel Bahaa goes to his refrigerator and pulls out a bakery box, the one picked up earlier on the patrol. He grins broadly. "I have just a little thing for your birthday." A cake from Haifa Street is hardly a little thing. I am delighted. "Take it with you so your team can celebrate." We save it for the next day. My mother has taken to celebrating birthday weeks in recent years. I think it is a shame she did not have this epiphany when I was nine. Nevertheless, thirty-nine will do.

So tonight, we sat out behind one of Saddam's old palaces. In the gardens under the palm trees are a variety of tea shops and small restaurants catering to the soldiers. We drink chai and eat cake. My team has been together for six months now. We laugh about those first few months of training, and plot the first few months of our return. Colonel Bahaa's gift takes us away, at least for a few hours, from a city still desperately in need of our efforts, tentatively embracing a few early rays of light.

RANT #1: 7 April 2007—War's Song

I have been in a crabby mood this week and feel the need to rant.

Apparently, I fell asleep during one of the most important classes in all my military schooling. It seems that it is possible to actually vote to end a war! To make matters worse, none of my peers in this army or in any of the others I have worked with bothered to let me in on the secret. I feel rather cheated. We can vote to stop a war and all my friends and I could come home. Hurray for us! It is like the best of *American Idol*. We get tired of the song we are hearing and we get to vote the singer off the show.

The early rounds of this war's competition were easy. It was not at all difficult to vote the 9/11 hijackers off the island. They were just plain evil. Afghanistan? That is like voting that William Hung fellow off the show. It is very easy to get on board with that vote. Saddam, yes, he could not carry a tune. Send him away. Sectarian violence in Iraq? Well, maybe we should let them stay for the next round. That group is almost as good as the free and democratic Iraq. We need to hear more to be sure. Only problem is, Simon and Paula do not get to make this cut. It has been tossed out to the whole world for a vote. Great big chunks of the world do not like the sounds coming from a free Iraq. The discordant notes of radical Islam play much better in the ears of many. The simple truth of the matter is that they too have a vote in this war, and for better or worse, they have chosen to engage us in Iraq.

Starting a war may be a matter of legislation but ending one is not. Once Pandora's Box is open the forces must run their course, and that means that the terms victory and defeat have to enter war's vocabulary. Ending a war involves only those two options. A tie you ask? Not in war's vocabulary. You might have a truce, a cease-fire, a lull, but eventually the issues that led to war will resurface, and it will play itself out. One side is going to get what they want and the other will eventually decide to either embrace the new ideas or die.

Ultimately, people fight wars over ideas. Sometimes they fight over small ideas like who should own this chunk of land or that one. However, the real big ones are usually over really big ideas. The Protestant Reformation, national socialism, communism were all major new theoretical constructs in their time that required an enormous toll in blood to resolve. Look at our own American Revolution and the ideas it hatched. After a grueling decade of conflict with the "insurgents" in the Colonies, England "voted" to give up the fight and withdrawl. However, ending the fight in the Colonies did not end the idea of democracy that was gaining momentum. Nor did it save England from having to engage in further warfare. Far from it, the ideas forged in our Thirteen Colonies jumped the pond to France, and by the end of that century, the French Revolution and subsequent Napoleonic Wars engulfed England and Europe in several more decades of warfare. What if England had decided that crushing the idea of democracy was worth the price?

What evidence do we have to support the theory that if we stop fighting radical Islam in Iraq that radical Islam will decide to accept the outcome of the vote and stop fighting us? They did, after all, start the conflict. Why stop now if they can run up the score? What pond will that dangerous idea jump? Unlike singing a duet, which requires two willing partners to participate, war does not. Failing to show up to the war when the other side is willing and anxious does not signal a desire for peace; it declares loud and clear your desire to be a victim. It signals that you are unwilling to put your ideals over the ideals of others. It demonstrates that you would rather find yourself alone under their rules, than risk danger and suffering to thrive under your own.

There was a time not too long ago when our nation's warriors sang when they went into battle and they unabashedly sang about their beliefs and values. The nation sang behind them. On this Easter morning, I am reminded of the lyrics of the third verse of "The Battle Hymn of the Republic," a very popular tune during our own Civil War:

"As he died to make men holy, let us live to make men free."

You know the tune! Let it roll around in your head for a little while … glory, glory, Hallelujah.

Increasingly the warrior class of our nation finds itself singing a cappella. Our military is more than capable of carrying the tune in a strong clear voice. While a cappella can be a powerful form of music, I find it generally sad, haunting, and fleeting. How much more powerful is a voice accompanied by the notes of even a single guitar? Feel the energy and tempo build with the steady rhythm of a drum! Let the power of the trumpet's call bring more voices to the song. Feel the energy of a choir as the original note, carried by that single voice, now carries a message of triumph and hope and victory! What songs do our enemies sing? What ideas fill their hearts when the war drums beat? We can vote to lay down arms, but we cannot vote to make their music stop. Turn off your TVs America. Pick up an instrument.

Update #10: 15 April 2007—The Clinic

A narrow sidewalk extends for about fifteen meters from the street to the door of a small health clinic that is just beginning to show signs of life. Either side is flanked by fruit trees that provide welcome shade in what is shaping up to be the first really hot day of the year. Together with the front gate, the trees block the view to the neighborhood outside. You could almost forget you were in the heart of what were killing fields three short months ago.

Outside the gates, American HMMWVs pack the street along with the blue and white National Police trucks. The street is remarkably clean compared to our first trip down here in February. The area is safe enough for trash trucks to enter, and the bulk of the refuse is gone. Shops are open again, not all of them, but enough to encourage folks out of their houses and to convince you that you are not living in a zombie movie. The buildings are still all riddled with the scars of gun battles, but some of the rubble has been moved. Particularly around a tiny, little blue domed mosque that had been buried when several hovels collapsed in on it.

Guards still occupy the ground floor of the maternity hospital a block away. We have been unable to get the Ministry of Health to support our efforts adequately enough to reopen the hospital. We are having better luck at one several miles away. You would like to think that it would not matter what sect a hospital belonged to, but sadly, it does. We have decided to try another approach. A local doctor has been adamant about doing something, so the U.S. brigade we work for is supporting him in opening a clinic. We are there to guard the first major event. The U.S. has done most of the work getting supplies and bringing in military medical personnel and assets to help open the clinic. My team along with the police of 5th Brigade are there to interact with the population and to get the word out that it is safe to come.

It does not take long for a crowd to form. Like a flock of crows, the black clad women of the neighborhood emerge with brightly feathered offspring on hips or in tow. They patiently wait in line to be treated, and gladly give up the offspring who flock to the Americans.

"Inteenee Football?"

"Inteenee Chocolate?"

"Inteenee flag?"

"Inteenee pen?"

Give me, give me, give me.

We hold back the goodies at first, and eventually the begging subsides. Photos are a good substitute, and they delight in seeing their images in digital cameras. Someone teaches the boys how to thumb wrestle, and eventually to arm wrestle. I make it a point to lose to all the boys under about eight and to beat all the older ones. The little ones love it; the older ones catch on quickly and revert to asking about footballs.

The mothers file through the clinic and emerge with medicines and ointments. Men venture out briefly to talk with them and ask questions, but largely stay indoors. No men between the ages of about fifteen and thirty-five are in evidence. They are still afraid the police will round them up and drag them away.

Colonel Bahaa and I engage in a near ceaseless dialog with the old men and the women folk as they come out and ask about electricity, missing loved ones, and any number of rumors. Two parts fear and one part hope, it is a constant battle to convince them that we really are working to make things better. They all admit that things have improved greatly in the last few months, but the despair of December and January is still very fresh in their minds.

In one particularly difficult conversation with three young women and the family matriarch of about seventy, they described their detained brothers and husbands.[6] Several were from years and months ago. I could do nothing to help. However, two happened several weeks ago. I recognized their names and was able to confirm that I had seen the men just days prior. When the women saw the names already written in my notebook, they knew that what I was saying was true. Having a seventy-year-old woman drop to the ground and kiss my feet is probably the most embarrassing thing I will ever experience. What an odd world to see unbounded joy in the face of a mother when she found out her son was in jail and not murdered.

Over in the corner, a scruffy old American print journalist is taking notes. I engage him briefly. He writes for a conservative magazine— *American Conservative* or some such, and the Marine Corps magazine *Leatherneck*. With him is a sketch artist, who is making a pen and ink drawing of the women waiting in line.

What I do not see participating is a single non-governmental health organization of any type. You would think that the International Red Cross could cough up a few volunteers for an effort as noble as opening a clinic in a war-torn nation. Especially after reading an article last week in which the International Red Cross made a scathing indictment of the conditions in Iraq. Apparently, they can find volunteers to write reports, but not to actually do anything about it. I guess Iraq is just too dangerous. This seems particularly odd to me given the roots of the Red Cross. If I recall correctly the International Red Cross had its first major human catastrophe on the fields of France during WWI. I do not ever recall reading that was a particularly safe place to be a volunteer.

It seems to me that war finds itself most often fought in areas where basic conditions are drastically out of balance between one group of people and another. If those who are most worried about achieving peace and goodwill (and the mission statements of most NGOs say something along those lines) fail to do anything in areas where conditions are most out of kilter, then why are the do-gooders critical of the military which

---

6   This neighborhood was predominantly Sunni. In the few months before our arrival, this area had been infested with a Sunni based Al-Qaeda linked organization called the Haifa Street Gang. They had recently been driven out by a combination of an American operation in February and increased pressure by the Jesh Al-Mahdi. As a result, many Sunni military age males either had been imprisoned or had fled leaving the female portions of the family to fend for themselves.

is the only agency actually trying to bring some sort of tenuous balance. I hear a lot of talk but do not see any action.

I read a lot, and one of my favorite authors recently is Paulo Coelho. In a book called *The Devil and Miss Prym*, he writes:

"I have two pockets, each contains a piece of paper with writing on it, but I only put money in my left pocket. On the piece of paper in my right pocket, I wrote: I am nothing but dust and ashes. The piece of paper in my left pocket, where I keep my money, says: I am the manifestation of God on earth. Whenever I see misery and injustice, I put my hand in my left pocket and try to help. Whenever I come up against laziness and indolence, I put my hand in my right pocket and find I have nothing to give."

That passage got me to thinking about all the times I have dropped money in a collection plate, or signed a payroll deduction slip to donate anonymously to some charity like the Red Cross. How many times have I given money from the left pocket to an organization that deserved right pocket treatment? When did just giving money ever really make me feel like I had contributed? What did I really change by giving money? How much more powerful to actually go and do something—to exert energy over time in direct contact with the problem that needs to be solved rather than abdicating responsibility to someone else to carry out goodwill on my behalf? The feeling I get when I drop cash in a collection plate is one of being finished. The feeling I get when I look in the eyes of a mother whose child finally saw a doctor for the first time in years is something more akin to "I have just begun."

A few years back, my group at the Army Staff College spent a day working with Habitat for Humanity building a house in downtown Kansas City. We all came back exhausted, but were much closer as a group, had made a bunch of new friends, and knew we had done something useful. It did not cost us a dime.

I get many letters from friends and relatives, and a surprising number of folks who I have never met who are reading forwarded copies of these updates. Many ask what my team and I need. The answer is nothing. However, here is what I would love to have. I would love to have a photograph of a house they helped build for someone who needs it. As of yesterday, it appears that we may find ourselves extended for another three months. That gives us almost another year. I wonder how many houses those readers could help build in a year?

Update #11: 23 April 2007— Awards

Voices echoed off the ridiculously tall ceilings of the palace. Unfortunate really, the intricate Moroccan designs carved into the ceiling are almost too far off to appreciate. I leaned up against the doorframe of a huge handcrafted wooden door with several other members of my team. We had been cooling our heels in a back room for over an hour and then hastily rushed to the lobby of the main conference room. The Iraqis hastened inside and the Americans were stripped off the tail of the procession as the large doors closed with some urgency.

Colonel Bahaa had been summoned to the Baghdad Area Command headquarters. All he had been told was that he was going to get some kind of recognition and he should bring Colonel Darfur and Lieutenant Colonel Abdulla, his two subordinate battalion commanders with him. Apparently, the command had decided that our district was doing the best out of the ten and they wanted to recognize them. You never quite know what that means in Iraq. In the past, it has usually meant a little bit of extra cash in the paycheck—like a Christmas bonus—only they do not do Christmas here. Given the years of Soviet influence, you would expect the Iraqis to all have chests overflowing with medals, but surprisingly they do not go for medals. At any rate, we had all figured it was going to be Lieutenant General Abboud Qanbar, the corps level commander giving the award. We had

73

met him plenty of times so we were all a bit surprised when we showed up to find security was much tighter than normal and everyone seemed on his or her toes.

Several minutes after Colonel Bahaa and crew disappeared inside, the door opened up again abruptly. A very serious looking western female complete with headset, burst forth, looked around, read name tapes, pointed at me and motioned me inside. I slid into line beside my counterparts, joined them at attention and let the eyes wonder while the ears got to work. At the head of the main table was Lieutenant General Abboud, the Iraqi commander of Baghdad. Chairing the meeting was the Iraqi National Security Advisor, along with the Minister of Defense, and the Minister of the Interior. Okay, this was a bit more that we had thought. No wonder everyone seemed so uptight today. Eyes continued around the table to the American side. Deputy division commander, check. Division commander, check. Corps commander, check. Gen Petraeus, grinning ear to ear. Yikes! It looked like King David had brought the whole galaxy of stars with him today. They all wore little earpieces. I would have been totally in the dark, but Miss Business took up a position behind my left ear and began translating loud enough that I could hear it as she spoke into the microphone connecting her to the other Americans.

The National Security Advisor lounged in his chair and swung to face General Petraeus. He then proceeded to tell a quick story about the first time he had met each of the three Iraqi officers, and a bit about the work they had been doing in our sector. Then he expressed his thanks to all the advisor teams that were helping his countrymen. The meeting ended. Petraeus vanished; a victim of what must be a punishing schedule. Handshakes all around, and a few minutes later, my group of dumbfounded colonels broke into laughter, all wondering what had just happened. An Iraqi aid bustled up, informed us that the actual "awards" would be in the mail, and trotted off. Needless to say, Colonel Bahaa was pretty pleased, and I could not have been prouder of them. They really have made a big difference in our area, even as things seem to blow up all around us.

Figure 23: Iraqi Minister of Defense Obdul Qadir, MNF-I
Commander GEN Petraeus and Major General Hussein, the
commander of the Iraqi National Police

We headed back to Colonel Bahaa's office. In the garden by the
front door, a wild female dog had been sheltering a litter of puppies.
They were weaned last week, and now the pack of seven grey and white
pups engaged in a never-ending rough and tumble. Iraqis normally do

not much like dogs, but they have been feeding this group. I think it is because they know that my team loves them. They call Major Koast the "adviser to the dogs." I head up the stairs and past the bloody handprint. It is starting to fade and I normally do not notice. I do today because Lieutenant Mahmoud is back on duty. He was the young bodyguard wounded in the car bomb attack. Mercifully he has full use of his leg again.

We lounge around in the office for a while, watching the news and sipping chai. Several of Colonel Bahaa's friends are lounging around. He gets all kinds of visitors during the afternoon lunch hours—old army buddies, family and community leaders. I expect something sweet to nibble on to come out any minute. I am hoping for a new treat called "windows" which has taken pole position from my old favorite "from the sky." Windows are a pretzel like pastry filled and covered with honey, making the window-like frame with gooey panes. Instead, I get a ver bitter pill. Major Koast comes in and whispers in my ear. "Doc just called. He needs you and Colonel Bahaa to come down to the detainee cage when you get a chance. We have some abuse." Crap. Have to wait for the guests to leave.

We check the detainees as often as we can and for good reason. Years and years of the Rodney King School of Law Enforcement has left most young Iraqis with a significantly different idea of what is normal than you or I would expect. We eventually make it to the cell and examine the twenty-some-year-old male. Doc slips me the statement the detainee wrote. I am not happy. The detainee's feet have swollen to twice-normal size. It would be several days before an X-ray could even be taken. I have little doubt what it will find. Colonel Bahaa and I have some words in private. I am particularly concerned about a young captain on his staff who proudly displayed a Muqtada al-Sadr picture on his wall until we made him take it down. "Accidents" always seem to happen on his watch. And for some reason a Shia's balance is genetically far superior to a Sunni's, or so I am told.

The mood is now significantly more somber than during the triumph of the morning. We start walking back to the office. The front gate of the compound swings open and a convoy of National Police trucks from one of our subordinate battalions rolls in. Shurta dismount in droves. We affectionately call the blue and white police trucks "clown cars" because you can really pack the shurta in. One

distraught looking civilian in business clothes gets out and five bound
hoodlums find themselves dumped unceremoniously onto the ground
and herded into the Intel section. An excited young captain approaches
Colonel Bahaa, stops the requisite ten paces away, drags the trail foot,
brings it up in a British style heel clinking stomp, while rendering a crisp
open handed salute. He then proceeds to fill us in on the latest action.

About an hour before, the distraught civilian had left his job at the
Ministry of Justice, and caught the bus home as he always does. An
SUV pulled up in front of the bus, stopped it, two men climbed on
board, grabbed the civilian at gun point, herded him off the bus, bound
him, put a bag over his head and tossed him in the back of the truck.
Fortunately, an astute Iraqi lieutenant at one of our checkpoints thought
something was up (the windows were tinted which is against the rules).
He searched the trunk and busted the attempted kidnapping. It takes
about an hour to get all the details and put the story together, but it ends
up being a very important catch.[7] Back on an emotional high.

♦   ♦   ♦

Several days later, I am in yet another palace with my friend. Equally
fine artisanship marks the walls and ceiling, and the sofas are the nicest
I have seen yet. Colonel Bahaa is under investigation for letting some
detainees go from our first big operation. We never should have taken
them in the first place, and letting them go was in order (I am willing
to bet that old Egyptian would agree with me on that particular point).
But, they happened to be of the Sunni sect, and so is Colonel Bahaa,
and that group is not in power, so people with friends call people, and
I got to spend the afternoon in the equivalent of the head of the CIA's
office helping my friend keep his job. Colonel Bahaa is as nervous
as I have ever seen him, but we still joke. I lean over part way into
the interrogation and whisper, "It is a shame that award has not come

---

[7]   This was the first significant capture of a Shia in the district since the
brigade took over in late February. It was a very visible capture by the Shia
dominated National Police and took place in a primarily Sunni area of the
district. In some ways, it marked a turning point in that neighborhood,
but would create some political problems for Colonel Bahaa.

in the mail yet! We may need it to bribe our way out of here." Four hours later, we make our escape. The file has been bottom drawered, probably to be miraculously rediscovered if advantage is ever needed. A shitty way to live, but probably the best we could have hoped for under the circumstances.

We drive back toward the headquarters, not much paying attention as we transit the "safe" International Zone. KRUMP. A wave of concussion rips through my belly. I am not sure why I always seem to feel concussion in my stomach. That was close, damn close. Every other time that I have been hit by artillery, I was out of the hatch. Stuck inside the HMMWV, with muffled radio headsets on, I felt the round far more than I heard it. I glanced at the driver, and he at me. I was just about to call the other truck to find out if they had seen anything when … KRUMP … a second round lands twenty meters behind my turned head. My driver and I are still debating whose eyes got bigger - mine, when I very definitely heard the explosion this time, or his, when he saw the debris block out the window behind my head.

A quick assessment and both trucks are fine, no civilians are hit, and the traffic on the busy traffic circle all continues to move. I call two rounds of 81mm fire into the tactical operations center. Colonel Bahaa and the other Iraqis riding in my truck jabber away in Arabic. Both are glad they were in the HMMWV and not a clown car. There is nothing like a near miss to put you back on top of life's roller coaster. I drop Colonel Bahaa off at his headquarters. We agree we have had enough for one day.

The mess hall was out of strawberry ice cream that night. Damn.

Update #12: 1 May 2007— General Order Number One

We rounded the corner at the bottom of the narrow descending street and into a now empty fish market. It was fast approaching eleven o'clock, and the fish trade is an early riser's game. The fish and the customers are mostly gone, but the smell lingers and hits us like a wave. We push through toward a black and red table surrounded by well-worn benches tucked up under a balcony. As we approach, the shurta fan out and an older man emerges from one the back rooms. All the movement sets aflutter a cloud of flies and it is suddenly clear that the table really is just red after all. I could not help but wonder if the flies or the smells were thicker.

We sat down to chat. Chai arrived. Chai always arrives. The day before, thirteen people had been grabbed from this market, forced into a truck, and driven away. Forty minutes later, the Shia captors realized they had raided the wrong market and took thirteen of their own. They released them. The Sunni market is about five hundred meters away and they had screwed up. If the stakes were not so high, the stupidity would be laughable. We talk in frustrating generalities. Hand waves. Them ... some people ... not sure what they looked like. All crap. The locals are either so scared they will not talk, or are supportive enough of the militia that they are willing to overlook what must have been a pretty terrifying abduction. Maybe both.

Colonel Bahaa is frustrated as well. We have had relatively little of the ethnic cleansing in our area recently, and this looked like a group coming from the outside to stir things up. He wanted to catch them. I notice a well-dressed couple walk by and wave. I recognize them from an interview a few weeks ago, a pair of Iraqi journalists from an AP or Reuters-like wire service. The woman has a flashy smile and a blatant feminist and Kurdish agenda. Her cameraman is well groomed and protective, but she is clearly in charge. They head our way, tell us that their office is just around the corner, and invite us up. Colonel Bahaa lets them know that we will be there shortly. A bit of a ladies' man, Colonel Bahaa is not about to miss the opportunity. We finish a bit of small talk with the fishmonger. We have to wait a bit longer. Colonel Bahaa has ordered me a fish for lunch, insisting I pick it out of the twenty or so remaining. It had been busy simmering in an old kiln-like oven trapped on a long handled iron fish-frying contraption. Eventually it is finished, wrapped and packaged with a variety of vegetables and pita for later consumption. We trudged uphill with more food than information.

I tossed the fish into my truck and got ready to head into the reporter's office. A muffled boom rings in the distance. It is hard to tell sometimes the size or distance when you are deep in the city. The buildings split and channel the sounds in unusual ways. It was far enough away that we were not in any danger. We ducked inside and upstairs into a well-appointed office. We engage in small talk about nothing in particular, and eventually receive an invitation back into a music studio. Local artists have been composing a song for each of the two national police divisions. They had just recently finished the verse dedicated to Colonel Bahaa's 5th Brigade and we are all delighted to hear about the exploits of the famous Sword Brigade putting fear in the hearts of the terrorists. Doc and my terp Victor began to dance, the enthusiasm of youth fueled by an attractive reporter with a flashy smile.

The second boom was much louder, and a wave of concussion left little doubt that this party was now finished. Everyone raced back to the trucks—game on. As the dismount team hustled back up the street, both Iraqi and U.S. truck crews plied the radio waves looking for info. The fish was discarded in the back as I piled into the truck and slid a headset back on. It took a few minutes to build a picture. Both explosions were in our sector. The smaller one, apparently a suicide vest, occurred at a café that the police like to frequent. The larger was a car bomb in a parking lot. We could see the smoke of the latter as we start winding through traffic that has gotten steadily thicker over the last few months. That day it was bumper to bumper in many places and the going was slow.

A mixed military convoy of Iraqi Army and Police pushed past us in the opposite direction, sirens blaring as they jumped into opposing traffic. In the bed of one of the police pickups was a blood-covered shurta with his leg propped up on the side. I say leg because there was no foot. I remember back to one of our forty hours of Arabic language classes. Apparently there is no separate word for leg and foot in Arabic. Absurd.

We arrived at the café about forty-five minutes after the explosion. If we had not known it had happened, we may have driven right past as we are so inoculated with war torn structures. Disturbingly, life was almost back to normal. There was no crowd, no onlookers; people shopped, kids played ... could this really be the place? It was. The storefront was mangled, the front window and door blown out, and an obvious pattern of debris from the center point. A pool of bright red blood made a disturbing pink color as it mixed in a slowly forming puddle of water produced by a neighboring shop owner hosing down the walls of his store.

We walked toward the building. A shattered cell phone lay in the street: hard to say if it or its owner took more damage. Six dead and another five wounded. The injured and most of the remains had already been removed. I stepped carefully preferring to look upwards and unwilling to analyze the crunching under my boots. In the shattered window on the second floor above the now rubbled café were the faces of two pre-teen children. Children should not look expressionless. It is not natural.

Several blocks away, a fire truck was finishing its chore of dousing the cars that were ignited in a secondary explosion from the car bomb. What could have been a much more spectacular attack was not. Mercifully, only one was injured. I would hate to be an insurance underwriter in this country. I was full of inappropriate thoughts that day. We rounded up several of the parking lot managers who were charging rent to use what used to be a public park. They came with us for questioning.[8]

The next day we are back to politics. Over the last few weeks, we have been garnering support for a reconciliation conference and have been parading around to various offices. The Governor of Baghdad is not doing too bad for himself, nor is the Director of Public Works. We check on a public school renovation project that the Governor promised us. It is ready to go. A project completely conceived, coordinated, and executed by Colonel Bahaa, without any U.S. help. He has been watching his American Brigade counterparts with a student's eye, and he learns fast. I am delighted, both by the progress and by the little cup of hot chocolate served in tiny antique porcelain mugs. This was a delicious diversion from the chai standard.

The days started running together. I soon found myself seated in a comfortable chair in the house of Dr. Chalabi of Iraqi National Congress fame.[9] Sadly, he was not present, and we were meeting instead with his staff to elicit sponsorship for our reconciliation conference. In one of the nicest neighborhoods I have yet seen, the house was not as large as I had expected but was immaculate on the inside. My mind drifted a bit as Sunni and Shia representatives from the neighborhoods in question vented about one outrage or another from the past few years. This placed looked exactly like the set of *The Brady Bunch*. Same bricks, same vaulted ceiling, same wood. I half expected Jan to flounce

---

[8]   We never did identify who was responsible for that day's series of explosions. We had not been in sector long enough at that point to have a well-developed set of sources, and the attacks directed against the fringes of the Green Zone often originated from outside of our sector, making them even harder to track down.

[9]   Ahmed Abdel Hadi Chalabi is a very controversial figure in both American and Iraqi Politics. He was one of the principal members of the Iraqi National Congress, which opposed Saddam Hussein from exile and provided much of the pre-war information about Iraq. He would later be investigated for questionable financial transactions associated with a bank in Jordan. Nevertheless, he has served in a variety of positions in the interim and current Iraqi Governments and was a key player in many of our interactions in the Karkh District.

down the stairs yelling "Marsha, Marsha, Marsha!" Hmmm where is Alice with the chai? I am parched!

A day later, I found myself back in the parking lot where the bombing had occurred. On the way there, we passed a car parked on the curb. Strapped to the roof was a pine coffin, decorated with the artful curves of Arabic script, memorializing the lost soul contained within. Ten to fifteen men and women from teen to octogenarian sat patiently on the curb waiting for some unknown event to kick off the procession. We were relatively close to where the suicide vest went off, and I wondered if this was one of the victims.

The lot is now all but empty. We have given orders to close it off. It is a weekend, so not a great test, but it appears that the police are enforcing the standard. The park is largely deserted except for the burnt hulks of last week's automotive victims. And the drunks. Drunks, you say? Yup, I was a bit surprised too. It was not yet noon. Nestled up into the weeping willow-like trees that dot the park are a variety of refreshment stands selling drinks out of coolers. Each has a handful of homeless bums huddled underneath. Clones of the ones you pass in New York, Paris, or Tokyo. They see us coming and all start trying to look busy by picking up cans, fixing abandoned auto parts that are well beyond repair, and trying to walk in a straight line. Colonel Bahaa shakes down the owners. Shurta search through the coolers to find hidden stashes. Captain Mundar, the commander of Colonel Bahaa's bodyguards, plucks a forty ounce can of beer from an ice chest. The can sweats as he pulls the pull-tab with calloused hands. Time stops. Staff Sergeant Ethington, Staff Sergeant Pettus, and I are trapped in a bizarre Budweiser commercial. Foam spills out over Captain Mundar's hand. He rears back and pitches the can in a high arch out toward the river. Amber fluid spills out and golden drops glisten in the sun as they fan out and rain to the ground. The Americans all look at each other, not sure who is going to cry first. The Iraqis laugh at us.

We follow the trail of illicit alcohol back to its source and find the mother lode. In a small compound, an outbuilding about five meters to a side overflows with crates of booze. All Arabic brand names scrawled in indecipherable text. However, the product is clearly displayed in English. Gin, Whiskey, Rum, and Beer. General Order Number One prevents U.S. forces from drinking alcohol and doing any number of other fun things. We are on the set of a classic war movie booze scene and the director has just yelled, "Cut!" Damn you General Order Number One! Oh well, its starting to get hot out. Booze would just dehydrate us and we have a lot of walking left to do today. Colonel Bahaa issues the appropriate warnings not to sell before 1600 hours and to keep it in the private confines of the casino, as the liquor license the owner possesses demands. We hurry off. This may be the first place we have been that did not serve chai.

Hours later we find ourselves at the other end of our sector, again down by the river. The lifeless corpse of a massive steel girder bridge lies shattered and half drowned in the Tigris. The bridge collapsed last week in a spectacular attack.[10] After several months of relative calm, the pace of attacks has picked up. Why shouldn't it? The enemy smells blood in our press and in the American halls of government. Evil thrives on fear.

Colonel Bahaa and I board a small river patrol boat, and the river police give us a tour. This is probably the single stupidest thing I have ever done. Colonel Bahaa and I giggle as the boat's captain takes us to full throttle and we bank hard and cut across our wake. A thousand summer safety lectures forgotten as camouflage body armor replaces orange life vests. We race past old riverside villas and a pair of jersey cows dining on river grass. The water is thick with silt, like last week's hot chocolate. I tell Colonel Bahaa about my family's lake house in Missouri and invite him to join me there in a happier future. We dock safely and weather the exasperated looks of my team. They all wish they could have gone boating too, but they enjoy the chance to call me an idiot just as much.

The morning after, we speed through a traffic circle we have passed a hundred times. At the corner sits an old vagabond woman we have dubbed the "crazy lady." Some days she dances for us when the traffic backs up. She sat quietly. Several blocks and minutes away we heard radio traffic on the brigade net. Apparently, a car bomb had just exploded at that traffic circle. We were all a bit surprised, as we

---

[10] The Sarifiya Bridge collapsed into the Tigris on 12 April 2007 after a suicide truck detonated killing 10 and injuring 26. This attack was part of a series of high profile attacks targeting transportation infrastructure. These attacks would cause major changes to traff

had heard nothing and were still relatively close. We found out later that it had detonated in a tunnel that cuts under one of the roads going into the circle, causing the road surface to buckle. Reports on injuries varied depending on the source. We have not had occasion to go back that way yet. Later that night, we sat in the garden outside the restaurants and video shops that fill one corner of our base. We sipped chai and talk about how crazy fate is and how much difference a few minutes make. The waiter collects the bill; he has been absent for the last few days. We learn that his brother died in a car bomb attack. We hope the crazy lady is okay.

Amidst all the loss in Iraq this week, I learned that a family member passed away. He was one of the last of my family's Greatest Generation. I hope that one day those two expressionless children from the second floor of the bombed out café will look back on these events. I hope that they will remember brave men like Colonel Bahaa and Captain Mundar as their greatest generation. I hope that we, like our grandfathers, always remember the importance of allies in a world that requires them.

I hope this letter finds you and yours disobeying General Order Number One.

Figure 24: Green's folly

Figure 25: Staff Sergeant Pettus and Staff Sergeant Ethington at the destroyed bridge

Update #13: 9 May 2007— Perserverence

I would complain about being hot, but I know that the worst is yet to come. After several months of remarkably pleasant nights and reasonable days, our grace period is up. At a mere 104 degrees, everything is incrementally harder. The only real mercy is that it remains light out longer, and the pace of life in the Mid-East adjusts to the brutal reality.

We make the turn off Haifa Street and into one of the poorer muhallas.[11] Three months ago, this wide side street would have been completely empty of all but trash, stray dogs, and a few men busy getting from one place to another. Two months ago, elder males would have been eager to tell us about their woes. One particular shop owner made a point of stopping every American patrol that passed in those first weeks and bringing them to his shop. Off his shelf he would take one of about twenty cans of various foodstuffs. The can had a bullet hole in one side and out the other. Proof of the "sniper," that hunted by night in the high rise apartments that overlooked the slums. An

---

[11] A Muhalla is a political subdivision of a neighborhood. In Baghdad, each Muhalla had a number, and 4-6 muhallas would typically make up a named neighborhood. 6-10 neighborhoods made up a named district.

all too real urban legend, the sniper boogey man, struck fear in the neighborhood and kept them out of the main street and tucked in the relatively secure back allies. Coupled with the corpse like hulk of the burnt out power station on the other side of the neighborhood, the residents told a constant and unrelenting tale of horror. Last month, the sniper threat had stopped as some of the cancer in the local forces was carved out in a series of arrests. People ventured back out in the streets and children became commonplace.

Now the people pack the street for the almost nightly game of soccer. The late afternoon cools off significantly and the last few hours of the day see families enjoying themselves at every doorstep, in the cafes, at the slowly improving parks and gardens, and in the streets. The crowd parts as we pass by during a joint patrol with our shurta. We weave in and out of the makeshift rock goal posts and through the slums. In another few hours, when we pass through again, curfew will be in effect. The streets will be empty, and most of this area will be dark. The electrical corpse here has yet to be resurrected.

Figure 26: Slums behind Haifa Street

However, the next neighborhood tells a different story. This area, while still a ghetto, is nowhere near as ancient as the one we have just left, nor has it suffered quite as much recent loss. Its infrastructure has been easier to replace, and neon signs and well-lit shops are gearing up for the setting of the sun. The streets teem with people and our fourteen vehicles wind through as if on parade. In May the almost enthusiastic greetings from entire families replace the tentative waves of February's children. Women who once discouraged kids from interacting with us now smile and wave. Males eagerly take the newspapers we drop off. Hard to say if they believe the government newspapers, but they are at least considering them. We still get hard stares from many. Knots of young males glare from street corners. Older men study us as we go by. Many still hate us, but terror's fever has largely broken and fled the neighborhood.

At the end of the block we recognize two of the local government leaders from our weekly council meetings. We pull over and dismount to chat with them. Colonel Bahaa, Major Brede and I chat on the corner while the nightly block party swirls around us. The frosty reception Colonel Bahaa received by the local governing council at our arrival in the sector surrenders to warm greetings and genuine appreciation. Months ago, the conversation was dominated with a list of demands about plugged sewers, mounds of trash, downed power lines, missing relatives and abusive security forces. Tonight, over a cold orange soda hastily offered by a local vendor, they eagerly tell us of the work that has gone on the last few days. Junker cars towed away. Water pipes repaired. Increased hours of electricity. They are beginning to see that cooperation with security forces allows for real work to happen. When real work gets done, people are happy. Happy people are happy voters. And happy voters don't shoot at us.

As we stood there, the shurta passed out newspapers. Many of the young kids took them, anxious to have anything free. One tiny young boy, barely pushing two, decided not to find himself left out. Smart enough to know that the papers probably originated from the Americans and not the National Police, he gathered up his courage, strode up to Major Brede, executed a flawless parade ground salute, stomped his heel in Iraqi style and asked in a clear young voice if he too could have a newspaper. One of Colonel Bahaa's security detachment quickly retrieved one from the many they handed out while our terp filled us in on the young lad's request. Major Brede presented the young trooper his trophy. If I could have one untaken photo from my trip here, it would be of that young child saluting the American soldier.

I will not be so naïve to say that all is rosy. The violence still rages all around our sector and, as last week reminded us, also in ours. Nor will I say that those men on the street corner have been converted. It is, however, progress that they are at least showing signs of being conflicted. Unsure if they should jump fully on the winning team, or if they should hedge their bets and keep one foot solidly in the enemy camp just in case worse comes to worst. These men walk a fine tight rope. Why shouldn't they? They read a steady diet of defeatism in the press and the endless stories about the upcoming September report to Congress.

I cannot help but wonder about the burst of energy the enemy must feel after years of climbing, knowing that they are no longer looking at a false peak. There it is! The summit is right in front of them! I have climbed enough mountains to know how easy that final ascent is. The burst of enthusiasm at knowing the end is in sight. After years of constant conflict, in a brutal strategy of pure attrition, this must be a huge relief. They had no measurable way of marking success; no march across Europe, no castles to siege, no flags to plant on an enemy capital. There is only an endless series of explosions and ethnic killings with no way of knowing when victory might be in sight. Now, completely inexplicably, we have told them where the finish line is. Foes who thought they were in a marathon know that they only have several hundred more meters to run. Those on the fence have renewed hope. Victory is in sight.

I wish my grandparents were still alive, or my parents were old enough to remember D-Day. I would love to know how they felt on hearing Eisenhower's powerful D-Day message.

Soldiers, Sailors and Airmen of the Allied Expeditionary Force!

You are about to embark upon the Great Crusade, toward which we have striven these many months. The eyes of the world are upon you. The hopes and prayers of liberty-loving people everywhere march with you. In company with our brave Allies and brothers-in-arms on other Fronts, you will bring about the destruction of the German war machine, the elimination of Nazi tyranny over the oppressed peoples of Europe, and security for ourselves in a free world.

Your task will not be an easy one. Your enemy is well trained, well equipped and battle hardened. He will fight savagely. But this is the year 1944! Much has happened since the Nazi triumphs of 1940-41. The United Nations have inflicted upon the Germans great defeats, in open battle, man-to-man. Our air offensive has seriously reduced their strength in the air and their capacity to wage war on the ground. Our Home Fronts have given us an overwhelming superiority in weapons and munitions of war, and placed at our disposal great reserves of trained fighting men. The tide has turned! The free men of the world are marching together to Victory!

I have full confidence in your courage and devotion to duty and skill in battle. We will accept nothing less than full Victory! Good luck! And let us beseech the blessing of Almighty God upon this great and noble undertaking.

SIGNED: Dwight D. Eisenhower

How sad that General Petraeus could not pull this speech off the shelf in its entirety. Unfortunately, the third paragraph needs some serious work, but this is 2007 and much has happened since Al-Qaeda's triumph of 9/11. We have inflicted serious defeats on the enemies' capabilities. Our home front? Well, ok we do not have a funding bill. And the freedom loving nations of the world? Well, ok they have lost their stomach. And victory would be cool and all, but ... you troops, you guys rock! We love you. Go knock yourselves out. You have about three months to pull a rabbit out of the hat. Do not screw it up.

The note that Eisenhower did not publish, the one he kept in his pocket, written before the operation in case of failure, read:

Our landings in the Cherbourg-Havre area have failed to gain a satisfactory foothold and I have withdrawn the troops. My decision to attack at this time and place was based upon the best information available. The troops, the air and the Navy did all that Bravery and devotion to duty could do. If any blame or fault attaches to the attempt it is mine alone.

What an incredibly amazing document. The commander on the ground in charge of the free world's human and industrial treasure took personal responsibility for success or failure knowing he had the backing of his government and its people—Great big brass balls!

Can you imagine if we had put the D-day invasion up to a congressional vote? How about the A-Bomb? How much harder would

D-Day have been if every aspect of the strategy had been second-guessed on every nightly talk show and editorial for months on end? Rommel would have giggled like a schoolgirl.

While I would never advocate a restriction on a vigorous public debate, the simple reality is that there is a time and place for the doors of Congress to close. The hard decisions to commit or withdrawl troops should be done in secrecy. And in a way that keeps the troops certain that the sand on the beach is worth wading up onto, keeps the enemy uncertain of how high the climb is, and keeps hope alive in the millions of tyranny's' victims who have a vested interest in which way the tide will turn.

Our job gets harder every day, but it is no less rewarding. This morning we drove past construction crews already rebuilding last week's collapsed traffic circle. The crazy lady has been forced to pick a new corner to sit on, but she is alive. I am left to wonder whose world is crazier, her's or mine.

Update #14: 18 May 2007—Car Bomb

"Slug bug orange, three o'clock!"

"That's three points, Ares Eight."

"Six this is five, did you see that one?"

"Roger, it was tucked in an alley, three points."

Three points put truck three's Sergeant First Class Babb just barely in the lead for the day, and the patrol was almost finished. I doubt that when any of us were nine, we would have predicted that we would still be playing "slug bug," but at age thirty-nine its every bit as fun as it was then. I am sure some will be appalled to hear that we scan constantly for the infamous Volkswagen Beetle as we drive the neighborhoods, but we do. We scan for lots of things: IEDs, cars from the BOLO (be on the lookout) list, people who are out of place, civic projects that are going on, and anything that is different from the day before. We look for patterns. After three months, we know where almost every VW Beetle in our area parks. So much so, that the lead truck was getting all the points because they knew where to look and always got first dibs as we rounded a corner. We have since had to adjust the rules, with trail vehicles getting more points than the lead. On most days, the occasional mobile slug bug will decide the score. For whatever reason all the bugs here are white or orange. Think we will add bonus points for other colors, just to keep things interesting.

"Six, this is Five, they are turning left up ahead."

"Tally Five."

That is odd. Why would they be turning in there? They must have gotten a call. Indeed, Colonel Bahaa's shurta had turned into an alternate road to avoid the congestion at the main intersection up ahead. The road is tight, so his trucks slip through where our HMMWVs barely fit. They race ahead, and we lose them. Something urgent must be going on. We finally catch up, Shurta have dismounted and are securing an area around one of our checkpoints. We park and dismount, moving up the line of vehicles to the far side of tall concrete barriers that block much of the view.

As we walk up through the search lane, it becomes apparent what has happened. A small car bomb has gone off. Obvious but not damaging scorch marks and debris advertise the area of detonation. The car, an old rusted-out red four door, continued to roll for another thirty meters out of the checkpoint and into a field next to the road. The car is intact, other than the shattered glass, and slight scorching. It is not on fire, and the only thing that would really distinguish it as out of the ordinary is the leg sticking straight out of the driver's window. I think it was Alice of Wonderland who first said "curiouser and curiouser."

Colonel Bahaa strides up, flanked by his guards. He has been on the radio since the first report, now ten minutes old, and has had an opportunity to assess the scene. An adult male in the passenger seat had offered to give a ride home to two co-workers from the International Red Cross (Note to self: IRC apparently does work here in Iraq after all). When the vehicle was driving out of the checkpoint, a small explosion from under the driver's seat ripped through the car, killing the driver. The man in the passenger's seat was slightly injured and the police already evacuated him to a nearby hospital. A woman in the back seat had been completely unharmed, other than being very obviously shaken. As we interviewed her, I was amazed to see that she was completely unmarked by either shrapnel or flame. Every hair was still in place, makeup still perfect.

Figure 27: VBIED outside of 5-2NP HQ near Muthana airfield

Normally we would assume that the attack was intended to harm the shurta at our checkpoint, but the very small size of the blast left us with the conclusion that it must have been designed to kill the driver. As we talked our suspicions over, the family of the man began to arrive. His brother, in anguish, was desperate to remove the body and take it home. Arabs are emotional about the issue of their dead, and Colonel Bahaa wanted to oblige, but we could not be certain that there was not another bomb in the car. We were going to wait for the Explosive Ordinance Disposal (EOD) to come, and the relative would have to wait.

More relatives arrived, and a crowd from the neighborhood began to form. The family was not at all pleased with being held at bay. The female victim waited patiently to the side, away from the driver's family. Eventfully one of her relatives arrived to take her home. As she departed, some of the dead man's relatives jumped into cars prepared to follow her. Colonel Bahaa barked a set of orders, and his guards quickly surrounded the cars. Had we not stopped them, she almost certainly would have found herself targeted in the strange cycle of revenge that always seems to taint what goes on here. She had survived where their brother had not, so she must be guilty.

The neighborhood crowd became agitated. This particular area is just out of our responsibility and is a security challenge. Someone over there took the opportunity in the confusion to act.

CRACK, CRACK, CRACK. Three AK-47 shots rang out. There was no indication of where they were aimed, but clearly a challenge to our authority.

Colonel Bahaa's normally rapid speech kicked into hyper-drive as he issued orders to his troops. His shurta all chamber a round and click their rifles onto fire. They formed a skirmish line along the road, taking a knee and aiming at the neighborhood. I almost wish Colonel Bahaa had a sword; it is the only thing that would have added to the effect. In a voice that projected across the field and into the neighborhood where the agitators gathered, he proclaimed loudly, "I have a thousand rounds for every round you fire. Go to your homes now." Colonel Bahaa, like most Iraqis, is fond of hyperbole. His words, backed by thirty rifles, proved sufficient to end the confrontation. The crowd dispersed, and the family lost much of its grief-born bluster.

We waited for EOD who were taking a long time coming. Each new family member who arrived begged Colonel Bahaa to let him or her take the body from the car. The anguish was palatable. They would rather die themselves, than fail to follow the traditions that they felt honor demanded. The Colonel stuck by his position. Too many people die here every day to take the risk. We would wait. And wait.

Lieutenant Mahmoud (the young man whose wounding prompted the bloody handprint) approached Colonel Bahaa. He was clearly upset, and had gathered all his courage to plead the civilian's case knowing that it would be a challenge to Colonel Bahaa's authority. The young lieutenant was desperate to help the family and honor their traditions. Letting the body just sit in the car in such an unnatural way was painful to them in a way that words do not quite convey. Colonel Bahaa loves Lieutenant Mahmoud like a son and talked quietly to him. The Lieutenant backed down, eyes tearing.

A few more minutes pass. The radio crackles. EOD will not be coming. We do not get an explanation why. The family wants to go get the body. Lieutenant Mahmoud will not hear anything of it. If someone is going to risk going out to the car, it will be a soldier and not those he protects. He picks five of his men. Doc fishes up some plastic gloves for them while they retrieve the pine box the family has brought. Lieutenant Mahmoud carries out his grizzly task while the rest of us watch with bated breath muttering whatever prayers our respective gods require.

They place the body in the box, and the Lieutenant leads the detail back to a waiting ambulance. The family begins to wail and console themselves as they take possession of their tribesman. Tears fall, mixing indistinguishably with the first drops of a light summer rain.

Figure 28: Lieutenant Mahmoud

"Inteenee chocolate!"
"Inteenee football!"
"Inteenee pencil!"
"Mister Mister!"

Give me, give me, give me! You guessed it; we are surrounded by children again. We are back in one of our favorite areas – the neighborhood with the sniper's can and the old Egyptian. Neither gentleman is present today, but many others are. The normal cast of characters gathers on the outside gates of a small local mosque pulling security. Inside, a team of Iraqi doctors is immunizing children for measles, mumps, rubella, and polio. I am particularly pleased to be out here today. The previous medical operations I have described have all been American conceived and resourced, with Iraqi help. This one is all the 5th Brigade's doing. After coordinating with the mayor, and Ministry of Health, Colonel Bahaa arranged for the event. He invited us along the night prior; it is the first I knew of it. No other Americans are involved—progress.

We chat with the locals and spar with the kids. The dismount team avoids giving anything away early. We know better. The kids know we have stuff; they just have to wear us down. Parents wait patiently in line. Several come and talk with us about one detained relative or another. One young boy named Haydr always makes a point to find me. He speaks great English and likes telling me about his school and his very strict English teacher. When I saw him last, we were talking with the local teachers about what renovations they needed. Today he came and told me all the things that workers repaired in his classroom: paint, new tiles in the bathroom, a sink that works, and air conditioners! Sadly there is not enough power yet to make them all run. Electricity, not the enemy, is our biggest barrier to further progress.

Another pair of boys approaches. I know them too. They are the most devious beggars of the lot. I am sure they have been harassing my guys up in the trucks, and the team has sent them down to bother me.

"Mister, give me football."

"Do I look like I have a football? Do I have magic pockets?" A shurta scurries him off. Another shurta brings up a falafel (a sort of Arab taco) that Colonel Bahaa has ordered. You know what that means. Chai is on the way too! While I eat, I call Staff Sergeant Ethington over. "Doc, go up to the trucks and get me one large trash bag, and a soccer ball. You want some of this thing? It is pretty good." He trots off shaking his head, leaving me to my culinary bravery, and returns several minutes later with a garbage bag in hand and a deflated soccer ball hidden under his body armor. Major Brede is with him with a cache of stuffed animals that Major Koast's family had sent.

I scan the crowd for my beggar friend, who obeys my summons. Victor translates my instructions. "You are too old to be begging, so I am going to put you to work. Take this trash bag, and fill it with trash. When you bring it back, I will give you a soccer ball." He gives me a funny look, not certain if he should give up his life of ease for the evils of a thing called work, but the temptation of a brand new leather orb is too much. He snatches the bag from my hand and races off, quickly attracting a flock of others. We watch as they begin to pick up smaller pieces of trash. They hold a quick conference. Small trash does not fill a bag quickly. Look for bulk. Eyes scan … cans, bottles … aha! A big box. It goes in unsmashed. Minutes later, the out of breath posse approaches, hoping to proclaim the task complete. I open the bag to inspect, and push down hard, flattening the empty boxes. The bag is half-full. Colonel Bahaa smiles and informs them they fell short of the standard. Young eyes roll.

Colonel Bahaa and Major Brede hand out stuffed toys to the smallest and most fearful of the children in line for the shots. Appreciative parents smile and nod. I have also armed Colonel Bahaa with a bag of peppermint candies, which he gives to each child as they leave, curing more than one frowning face. I catch him sneaking one for himself. One very old grandmother emerges with three young ones, each eager for a treat. She gives Colonel Bahaa a toothless grin, and asks if she gets one. With eyes that twinkle like old Saint Nick, he offers her one. She may have been the happiest of all that day. Minutes later, task complete, my small work party makes off with their prize.

Meanwhile, up at the trucks, the battle for stuff is raging in earnest. Every time one of my guys opens a trunk, a crowd descends on them. Sergeant First Class Carrejo braves the masses to recover a box of stuff my sister sent—a bunch of notepads and packs of crayons that we had bagged up. Knowing chaos will ensue, he hands them up into a truck full of shurta to distribute. They do not have much more luck at controlling the kid swarms than we do, but they at least can speak the language. The small packages are a hit. Most find hiding spaces beneath shirts or are quickly policed up by mothers to end ownership disputes.

Two hundred immunizations later, we finish. War should not be fun, but sometimes it is.

Several hours later, back at the compound, I was eating a very late lunch with Colonel Bahaa. The reporters I have mentioned previously had come to deliver the final version of the brigade song they had composed. Much of the conversation was lost on me, as all the terps were out and about with the guys finishing up some business. I have not mentioned the terps much lately, which, given their importance is a gross oversight.

We have lost several of our original group. Rafid, the atheist engineer was under a lot of pressure from his new wife and left us to move down south. He calls us now and again, and he is doing well. He finally found a job with the ministry of Oil and is glad to be living in a much quieter region of Iraq than Baghdad. Gary the doctor has also left us. He is waiting for his approved visa to the U.S. to finally take effect, and with that elusive goal in mind, he decided that work with a team that was always going on patrol was too much of a risk. We found him a terp job that does not require him to be quite as active. We had one young man come and go; his English was not quite good enough, and our shurta were getting really frustrated because they knew something was amiss. We found him a job where a mistake was not as likely to get someone killed. Saki, the Armenian Christian is with us for a few more days. Much older than the other terps, and with a temperament much like Oscar the Grouch, he has become disenchanted with some of the team's shenanigans, and vice versa. After some long debates, we agreed that maybe he would be better off on another team, so we have found him a new home as well. I like the old guy and will be sad to see him go, but I did not have to live in a trash can with him.

That leaves us with Victor as the only one of the original crew. He is now the old timer and very proud of his position as lead terp. Young and cocky, Victor is very good at what he does. He is joined by Frank, who is also very good and who has been with us for about a month. So far, he has been very quiet around me, but he fits in well. Our final terp is a new guy named Snake. Snake is a bit of a character. A Kurd with a political science degree, he has been working as a butcher. Apparently that would not pay for his two wives and four children, so he is using his English for the first time in the terp trade. Unfortunately, his youngest son by his second wife (who is pregnant with a fifth child) has been ill lately. We gave him a few days to help the family while the son was in the hospital with a virus that had caused him to lose a lot of weight. Snake had returned to duty the night before, after the doctors released the child from the hospital.

As we finished up lunch, Major Brede poked his head into the room. "Sir, I need to speak with you a second." I excused myself. Colonel Bahaa gave me a questioning look. I am not anxious to air any laundry in front of the reporters.

"What's up?"

"Snake just got a call, his son died this afternoon."

Silence.

"Okay, get everyone kitted up, let's get him to his family."

I let Colonel Bahaa know what was going on and apologized for my hasty retreat. He explained to the others in Arabic as I departed. I hurried back to the truck. Back on the FOB the team gathered under the palm trees around the trucks. The terps all helped Snake pack and offered what comfort they could. The rest of us took up a collection; Snake had not yet reached his first payday and had borrowed money for hospital bills. We stood around quietly lost in our thoughts until he arrived for his ride out to the gate. Many on the team have children and witnessing our worst fears had us all a bit shaken. Snake arrived. A thousand words exchange silently in the form of an embrace, or a gentle nod, or a hand on the shoulder. He drove off. He may not come back. I certainly would not blame him if he did not. Either way, he is one of us now.

It had been raining. I almost failed to notice.

Figure 29: Naws Najim Abid " Frank" at FOB Prosperity

Figure 30: Snake

Update #15: 28 May 2007— Heroes

We are back in the palace waiting patiently in the entry hall. A worker is mopping the Italian marble floors, which reflect the dim light of an enormous chandelier that hangs from the carved Moroccan ceiling three stories above us. We moved around from one side of the chamber to another twice already, photographers and assistants trying to figure out the right location for the ceremony. As is true of most things here, the exact nature of the ceremony is a matter of some conjecture. The night before, Colonel Bahaa informed me that we had to be here at 8 a.m. with six members of his personal security detail for an awards ceremony. Later that night while sifting through a stack of emails, I found one that shed a small amount of light. Buried in the thread is a comment from General Petraeus to Major General Odierno saying he will be the one to give out the awards, but there is little meat on the bones other than that. Given the names of the shurta involved, Lieutenant Mahmoud, Gazi, Nabil, Mohammad, Nour Adin, and Daud, I can only assume it has to do with the car bomb from a few days ago.

A suit walks up to me, an earpiece stuck in his ear. He looks about my age and out of place in a coat and tie. He clearly knows who I am and without introductions gets straight to business. A flurry of words are exchanged. "Do you know what this is all about? ... great story ... read your report ... chance to recognize heroes ... the General will be here shortly ... how do we pronounce this name ... great stuff ...” Then off he goes leaving me with little more knowledge than I had other than confirming my suspicions linking the incident to the ceremony. My mind races back to the official report I sent, which as I recall, was far less detailed than the account I gave in my last letter; so much so that I am left wondering if my update, and not the official report, is the basis of the day's event.

Regardless, a crowd began to gather around the six shurta who stood at a loose form of attention in front of the Iraqi, American and Brigade colors. Colonel Bahaa fussed over them. They all wear the same uniform, the old American style green battle dress uniform. On most days, these six would probably sport at least three or four different camouflage patterns. Today they have borrowed what they needed and look uncommonly uniform. Colonel Bahaa is a bit of a traditionalist in terms of uniforms. He thinks military uniforms should be green and that the appropriate headgear should be the beret. He has found a red beret for each. Anyone who has ever worn a beret will know that you just cannot borrow one from someone else. They are temperamental creatures. Some take months of training to conform properly to the head. The shurta fidget uncomfortably trying to keep them on. Their eyes wander as they admire the palace they never could have imagined visiting.

The pace quickens when the important people start arriving. Major General Hussein, the general in charge of the National Police is early and looks over the troops. The MND-B commander, Major General Fil arrives followed by my brigade commander, Colonel Roberts. The Minister of Interior, the Corps Commander, Lieutenant General Odierno, and the Minister of Defense enter the hall. All are here for a meeting after the ceremony. Colonel Bahaa, Colonel Roberts, and I move outside to greet General Petraeus when he arrives. He is all smiles when he pulls up, and after exchanging brief greetings, focuses straight in on Colonel Bahaa and gets to work. They have a quick discussion about expectations and standards and the status of our Karkh Security District. Then it is inside so the fun can begin. I slinked off to the side and joined my team to watch. Colonel Bahaa falls in on the end of his row of shurta.

The ministers gave a few quick words describing the bravery of the young men willing to risk themselves to protect their countrymen. General Petraeus did much the same, and then they began to load the awardees down with gifts. From the Americans, a certificate and a coin. For those who do not know, the unit coin has almost replaced the traditional medal as a form of recognition. Each unit commander develops a coin with unit crests, mottos, and histories, which they present to soldiers. It requires no paperwork, is immediate, and usually much more valued than the official ribbons. The shurta love it. Several have started wearing plastic ID card holders on their arms and have the coin tucked inside for all to see. The Minister of Defense is generous as well. An official letter accompanied by a gift of 500,000 dinar (about $350) and a promotion of one rank. Seeing themselves on TV that night or in the newspapers over the next few days can hardly be discounted either. More words are exchanged as the ceremony dissolved into the normal swirl of congratulations and mingling. I caught an occasional glance from the shurta. They wink and nod at my team. They were as proud as they could be. So was I.

Victor slid up next to me. "Sir, I think the Minister of Interior just told Colonel Bahaa that his promotion is approved. He handed him some official papers."

"Are you serious, they didn't announce that?

"Sir, that's what I heard him say."

"Wow, I better go find out."

When the crowd finally departed for the meeting and Colonel Bahaa and I are back in charge of our agenda, I ask. "So General, do you have something to tell me?" He grinned and his eyes sparkled. He took an envelope out of his breast pocket and unfolded the paper inside to show me. I did not have to read Arabic to know what it said.

Figure 31: COL(P) Bahaa and Major General Hussein surrounded
by awardees at Adnon Palace

◆   ◆   ◆

A few of my team gathered around the back of our HMMWVs. We watched silently. There was really nothing to say. Snake, our terp, stood spread eagle with his hands up against the truck. A squad of military policemen from the detention facility searched him methodically, cataloged his belongings and cuffed him. Snake was silent as well, and he complied. He did not attempt to make eye contact. Over the last few days, it had become clear that Snake had been serving as an enemy agent. We were lucky to detect it after only a few weeks. We have no idea if his infant son really died last week; we hope not for his wife's sake. We do know that the charity we gave to him will not be recovered. We are reminded that the first casualty of war is innocence, and trust has been wounded in the collateral damage.[12]

---

[12]   Snake spent several months in American confinement facilities before being released shortly before my team came home. He never provided any useful information to interrogators and we never saw him again. It is impossible to say if he was simply trying to turn over a new leaf, or if he was trying to work back into a position from which he could cause trouble.

Hours later, we are preparing for a mission. Captain Szkotnicki gave the intelligence dump before we rolled. He gave the details on an attack that happened the previous day. One of the transition teams we had trained with at Fort Riley was hit with one of the explosively formed penetrators (EFPs) that come from Iran. Two of our comrades were dead and a third very badly burned. The mood was somber. While many of the teams we trained with have been attacked, these are our first casualties. Today there is none of the normal cheerful banter and good-natured abuse we normally exchange as we head out. I got into the truck and strapped on my intercom set. Sergeant First Class Carrejo already had his on and commented quietly, "The team is pretty shaken up today, what can we do about it?"

"Yeah CJ, we are a bit shaken up. Nothing we can do but get back in the saddle. The war isn't going to win itself."

We of course will do something about it, collectively and alone. Pray, tell stories, listen to music, write. In a few days, we will attend the memorial service. Then, like generations of Americans before us, we will go back out and win. It is what our country expects, and it is what we expect of ourselves.

◆   ◆   ◆

I read an editorial today in the *Stars and Stripes* newspaper. A teacher asked her class what Memorial Day was. One young man apparently answered, "That's when the swimming pools open." Sad but true.

It is quite possible that young man's family has not had any members who served or died in our nation's service. Maybe there are no stories for him to hear, no family heirlooms on the wall, no uniform in the closet, no racks of medals on display, no photos on the mantel, or no grave to put a flag on. However, I doubt it. My guess is, no one took the time to tell him those stories. I also bet he would love to hear them and would be a better man if he heard them now as a boy.

One of my favorite possessions is a typed manuscript of my grandfather's autobiography. In it is a mix of stories that he told us as kids and some that he never really mentioned. Before I deployed, I reread his tales of service in the Navy Seabees during WWII and of recovering in a long string of veteran's hospitals when he returned home. I am grateful to have the opportunity to travel back with him, all because he had the generosity to leave that behind for us. It is largely why I choose to write these letters home. One day, when all is said and done, I hope that my girls can dust off my words as well. Memorial Day should be remembered with memories and not just a small flag next to a stone. Then, if it is really hot, maybe a dip in the pool.

Update #16: 8 June 2007—The House Guest

The room was dark and reasonably cool given that the power was off and neither fan nor air conditioning was contributing to the solution. "Peace be with you General."

"Ah, Lieutenant Colonel Green!" General Bahaa smiled and struggled to prop himself up onto an elbow. His operations officer had told me a few minutes earlier that the general was sick, but that he had asked that I come over to his house. I rounded up my medic, and headed over to his quarters. My team doc is on leave, so we have borrowed Sergeant Novatney for a few weeks to cover the gap. Young, competent, and enthusiastic, he fits right in. He grabbed a pair of Iraqi medics to come along and do the actual work.

Bahaa lay on a futon in his living room watching TV with his wife. Now that I think about it, I am not sure why the television was working while nothing else was. The Iraqis have made siphoning electrical power into an art form. At any rate, his wife made her exit as a slew of medics arrived to bombard the general with questions. He suffered it all patiently. Dehydration and exhaustion were almost certainly the culprits. For every patrol that we go on with him, he does a second. The last week has been stressful and he has had seven hours of sleep in three days. The medics all scold him in the way the medical

113

profession is allowed to do. He knows they are right. I sent them all away. He asked me to stay.

His wife returned with chai and the three of us talked quietly and watched some satellite TV. After a few minutes, his young niece of about thirteen scampered in and joined the group. A few minutes later the General's university age daughter came skipping down the hall and slid to a halt at the door in stocking feet, sweat pants and tee shirt. She panicked when she saw me sitting there and raced back down the hall. She emerged a few minutes later in a black robe and headscarf. Feeling much more appropriate, she joined the group. She had attended school until a year ago; now it is too dangerous. She is largely trapped in the house. Mom delegated the next round of chai to her. The General's seventeen-year-old son and nineteen-year-old nephew both come and go. The nephew is in uniform. He is actually one of Bahaa's shurta. The son is out of uniform today. While not officially in the National Police, he often wears a uniform, goes on patrol, and, much to my team's annoyance, frequently wears dad's rank when dad is not around.

We talked a bit of business. The General appeared to be perking up. He made the comment "I was just lonely." I laugh—because it might be true. Arabs are very rarely alone and Bahaa is usually surrounded by people who need something from him. His daughter came back in. She had shed the black coverings and was once again clad in sweats. Apparently mom or dad had declared me safe. We watched the five o'clock news. I recognize more of Baghdad and the local politicians now than I do of D.C. or my own policy makers.

The phone rings. It is Bahaa's oldest son calling from Syria. He has been there for several months. He had been serving in the army but was getting threats against his life based on his dad's position. He wanted to come home. Dad says "No." He tries to convince mom. No luck. She asked him to get a prescription filled for her that she cannot get in Iraq. Niece and daughter were trading video clips and songs on their cell phones. Dad heard something that peaked his interest and grabbed the daughter's cell phone and started watching. As he thumbed through it, nephew, niece, and daughter all exchanged guilty "uh-oh" looks. I could tell they are just waiting for dad to find something he should not. The young niece noticed my amusement and poked her cousin who all of a sudden looked doubly guilty.

Daughter checked her watch and pleaded with mom. The channel changed to the opening minutes of *Iraqi Idol*. Everyone settled in. Dad handed back the phone. Any contraband was either undiscovered or returned without remark. The first contestant was a young blind man in his early twenties. He sang in a deep slow voice that sounded much like the call to prayers we hear every day. The first song was a love song. When he finished Simon-Mohammad give him a hard time. Paula-Fatima propped him back up. The final judge, a friend of the General who works at the local university for the arts gave him a second chance and the young man launched into a second tune. This one he wrote himself. The General gave me a feel for the refrain. Essentially a blind man's desire to see the country he loves. Mom sobs audibly, wipes a tear, and whispers something in Arabic. Bahaa touches her softly. I asked if the song was that powerful. He replies, "No, she was friends with his mother; she is dead now." I retreated into silence, unsure how to reply in either English or Arabic.

Eventually I made an exit. The team had finished up our day's work outside and I had intruded long enough. For a few hours in a tiny portion of the city, for a very few people, life has been perfectly normal.

Figure32: MAJ Brede, Brigadier General Bahaa and his son Mustaffa take lunch in Bahaa's kitchen

◆   ◆   ◆

Three days into month six and the urge to count is starting to take over. We are almost at the halfway point, or at least hope so. The three-month extension does not appear to affect us, but we are all painfully aware that the shelf life on truth in Iraq is measured in hours. Three of the team have already gone on leave and returned. The fourth is home now and everyone is teasing Sergeant First Class King about having a bag already packed for his upcoming departure. My turn is still months away. It is too early to count that yet. Statistically, month's five to seven are the worst. That is when the guard comes down and complacency sets in. At this point we have done most of the things we are likely to be asked to do. The excitement of the first few months has worn off as tasks become routine and new places become old stomping grounds. That which was easy to fix has been done. That which is difficult is often really difficult.

Most of the team has started to get orders for follow-on assignments. The mind naturally drifts to planning events that cannot yet be influenced. It is still early enough to count off birthdays and holidays missed, and not yet far enough along to start planning the ones yet to come. The heat makes it worse. A few merciful hours in the morning or late at night bring folks out to socialize on their stoops. However, the heat of the day is exhausting mentally and physically. After a day of patrolling or meetings it is hard to wish for anything more than to disappear into an air-conditioned cocoon. All the music starts sounding the same. The names of the insurgents start running together. DVDs start moving back to the top of the play list as reruns. Another District Area Council meeting brings another complaint about the lack of electric power.

There are days when I feel like a crewmember of a becalmed ship. The classic movie scene with everyone sprawled out on deck with tongues dragging over blistered lips. The sun beats down and the hero paces because he has some place else he really needs to be.

We are making progress even if the wind does not always seem to be in our favor. We escorted Dr. Chalabi, a prominent political figure, on a walking tour of Haifa Street the other day. While it is starting to seem commonplace to us, it is still remarkable to have him stroll through about two and a half kilometers of back streets and markets. Film crews documented his tour and his conversations with shop owners and citizens. Those alleys were deserted a few short months ago. The main street is now lit by solar powered streetlights, a very visible sign of change. A local paper back in Texas, where our U.S. brigade is stationed, ran a story about the improvements. The headline recalled the street's former nickname: Purple Heart Boulevard.

For every action there is an equal and opposite reaction. The enemy still makes his evil presence felt. Just as in the movies we remain vigilant and wait for a sail to rustle or the music to strike up, letting us know that something more exciting is ahead.

Update #17: 21 June 2007—
Enemy Ground

"Six this is five, Bahaa is on the ground."

"Roger" pause …

We were not in one of our neighborhoods so a decision that had become almost automatic took several seconds to process. The night before the General had asked if I would come on a patrol with him the next morning to visit one of his subordinate battalions. His first battalion had not been under his command in the last six months. They have been up north and we had very little interaction with them. The previous day the unit had road marched down to Baghdad where they were going to take control of a new area freeing a unit of Pesh Merga from northern Iraq to return home. The first battalion would not be working in our sector nor would they be under our control. Nevertheless Bahaa felt it was his responsibility to go visit, see how the unit was doing, and give the battalion some advice on how to regain control of an area that had not made anywhere near the progress ours had. The fact that this neighborhood was where Bahaa had lived as a boy and during the interim between the invasion and his entry into the National Police was an obvious second motive.

As I expected, the news of our trip went over like a fart in church, but, to their credit, the team didn't say anything. This was not our area. We had never been there before and it really was not strictly our task.

However, the transition team that works with the first battalion had lost a truck to an IED a few days previously and they would not be there. I agreed with Bahaa that we should help the unit out on their first day in sector, so I decided to go. Bahaa had been unable to give me the exact grid that night and the map I had was not an appropriate scale to plan the route. We would work out the final details in the morning, but I was pretty certain that I knew where we were headed. It would put us into an area that was significantly more contested than that to which we were accustomed. Everyone went about the morning pre-combat ritual with a bit more urgency: the unknown being a remarkable cure for the corrosive effects of complacency. A few extra glances at the map … double checking radio nets … calling adjacent units to check route status gave evidence of concern. The shurta in the trucks in front of us looked a little more serious as well. It reminded me of a passage I had read in a book by Paulo Coelho a few weeks ago. "Fear reaches only to the point where the unavoidable begins; from there on, it loses its meaning. And all that we have left is the hope that we are making the right decision." I tucked that thought away. We were off again.

Within minutes, we plunged into the new neighborhood. The jitters were gone and the team quickly stepped up the cross talk, picking out unusual things and comparing them mentally with what we knew to be normal in our area. The urban geography was much different here. The streets were much wider, the houses almost all middle class and two stories. The streets were all laid out in a neat grid. They are much different from the ramshackle city planning and mix of urban high-rise and century old slums that dominate much of our area. A few things were immediately obvious. We did not see any regular Iraqi police, we ran into no other Americans, and the people were … cautious.

We made link up with the first battalion in their new compound. They were just settling in and had yet to get generators established. We sat in the battalion commander's hot, dark office while the two leaders talked. Outside the shurta from our brigade and the first battalion mingled in a family reunion of sorts. Many had fought together in Fallujah several years ago when the unit formed. Bypassing both chai and the traditional small talk, Bahaa went straight into business mode giving advice on how he thought Colonel Zuhir could best establish himself in the opening days. Shortly thereafter we were back in the trucks. Active patrolling by the commander is high on Bahaa's list of priorities. We were all going for a ride.

I had very little feel for what the history of the neighborhood or the ethnic makeup was, but it quickly became obvious as we weaved our way through the city grid. Most of the outskirts of the neighborhood were relatively normal; shops were open, there appeared to be a fair amount of electrical power and by and large the streets were clean. However, the closer you got to the area's main center boulevard the more things changed. At the north and south end of the mile long stretch stood barricaded checkpoints over watched by corner buildings that were sandbagged and fortified. The National Police now occupied positions that apparently the Pesh Merga of the Iraq Army had been in just days before. The center street was completely empty—not a soul to be seen. Trash was piled up in complete juxtaposition to the two roads that paralleled it just one block away. All the shops were closed—there was no life. I had seen streets like this before in two places: in zombie movies and in our own district when we had first occupied it back in February. This was an ethnic border battleground and, from the looks of it, the Pesh Merga had been turning a blind eye to whatever was going on, biding their time until their deployment to Baghdad ended.

As we left no-man's land and headed back into populated territory the commanders began to dismount and press flesh at local markets. I stayed in the truck. Americans have a way of pulling the populace to them and this was not my area. I would not be able to talk intelligently about anything that was happening here. Because they always assume you are lying if you say you do not know it is best not to give them the opportunity to ask. Besides, what was important here was getting Iraqis to trust Iraqis ... so we stayed mounted and watched.

Then the shooting started. It is hard to know how veterans can tell which shooting is dangerous and which is not—but they can. Both Iraqis and Americans are pretty inoculated to the sounds of far off gunfire, accidental discharges, or the occasional warning shot. However, for some arcane reason, when a shot is aimed at you ... you know! The first round alerted everyone's senses. Much like a prairie dog colony, turrets and heads all swiveled left scanning for danger. A bombed out high rise affectionately dubbed the "sniper motel" was the dominant piece of terrain some 800 meters away, but the shot was almost certainly from the palm groves and associated farm houses much closer in. Three more shots rang out in rapid succession and shurta sunk lower in their far from adequately armored trucks. To their credit, none returned fire. Many Iraqi units unleash a "death blossom" when they make contact, indiscriminately shooting in every direction. We could not identify the source of fire so did not return it.

Brigadier General Bahaa and Colonel Zuhir finished their conversation with the market owner. Personal bravery is a large component of Arab leadership. While leading from the front is certainly the norm in the U.S. Army, much of the power of American commanders comes from the ability to reach out by a network of communications systems and call upon a dizzying array of assets, quickly gather a picture of what is going on, and bring all the right pieces to bear. The Iraqi really has much more in common with our ancestors from the Civil War. In many cases, standing upright in the middle of things, barking orders, and acting unafraid is about the most useful thing they can do. I often think that if Bahaa had a horse he would mount up in a firefight just so his guys could see him better.

The fire stopped and he mounted his truck rather than a steed and we continued on our way. There were very few people in the main streets now, but many in the alleyways. As we headed south, we heard more shots. None of the fire appeared to be aimed, but it was following us, challenging our presence. As we got to the end of the block a group of civilians emerged from the shops and waved us down, pointing back up the side streets. They clearly had an idea of where the fire had been coming from … and that had enticed the general back out of his truck.

"Five, this is six, I am on the ground."

"Roger."

Major Brede and Captain Ly joined me as we formed up with the shurta. About fifty of them had dismounted and began to fan out, a small group off to each flank, while the main body started moving up the next side street. Major Koast maneuvered the trucks to over watch as we patrolled up the road. The road was deserted. We could see up it for almost five hundred meters and we began our advance. I could hear people inside their courtyards … moving indoors or locking gates. Each noise attracted the muzzle of a weapon. One man braver than the rest stood in his open courtyard gate and peeked out after the main group of shurta passed. My team was in the middle with a few of the heavy weapons brought up in support. I smiled "aSalam Alykum—peace be with you." In English, he replied, "You are welcome here." Interesting. We advanced further up the street.

Several hundred meters ahead a large house dominated the intersection. It had been fortified and almost certainly lived in by the Iraqi Army at some point. They are all gone now and the once proud house stands pockmarked with bullet holes and neglected. The shurta smashed in the front door and began to clear it. Within minutes, the General and his men are up top pushing off the sand bag positions, leaving it looking significantly less threatening. I moved inside the bottom floor. While the Iraqi Army has been gone for days, a lone mattress lay in the entry foyer with a small stove, kettle, and the remains of breakfast. Someone had clearly moved in already ... potentially our friend the gunman. This gave some credence to what the locals had told us minutes before.

We continued up the street all the way to the palm groves where we had first taken fire. As we had advanced north our vehicles had trailed in overwatch. The shurta led with a pickup mounting the largest gun in their arsenal. The DISKA is a huge Russian made anti-aircraft gun that dwarfs the American-made .50 caliber machine gun. It is a beast of a weapon not meant to be mounted in the ass end of a Silverado pickup truck. However, what is not meant to be rarely survives contact in Iraq and somehow they had mounted the gun into the truck. Having reached the limit of our advance the commanders decided to halt the pursuit. As the patrol began moving back south and the gun truck negotiated a three-point turn, our friend the gunman decided to take a final stab at us as we withdrew. A short burst of fire bounced off the pavement just behind the pickup. The startled crew spotted the gunman as he ducked into a house, and immediately threw the truck in reverse. A quickly shouted exchange from Bahaa to the gunner determined that he had positive identification on the house. Dismounted shurta took up the prone or ducked behind corners and the order to fire was muted in an impressive gout of flame and noise as the DISKA opened up, drowning out the accompanying PKC and AK-47 fire.

Much to my surprise, when the cloud of dust settled the DISKA was still mounted and the truck had not flipped over. Sadly, I was not in a position to see the condition of the target farmhouse. Two solid bursts later, the General was satisfied and ordered the withdrawal. An American unit would almost certainly have swept the objective, but I was not going to call him on it in front of his men so we made our way back to the trucks.

Back at the end of the street, the shurta received a warm reception, with previously cowering residents now emerging from courtyards with pitchers of water. One elderly man emerged with a dish of candy and began tossing them up into the trucks. We slowed down long enough to take a handful ourselves. A surreal turn of events considering how much candy we have passed out in previous months. As we continued off that street and into the next few blocks our reception continued to improve. The Iraqi commanders dismounted again, moved into a crowded marketplace, and talked with locals. This was Bahaa's old stomping ground and he introduced Colonel Zuhir to the locals and explained that things were going to change. Many recognized him from a string of TV interviews he had done the previous week. His newfound fame and a series of positive spots on the progress in Haifa Street were lending credibility to both commanders.

My team was surrounded by the inevitable mob of children. I tried to keep out of the General's way while he worked the crowd. Some days our role is much like a trophy wife. It is simply enough to stand to the side and be American. We lend an instant air of credibility. We added nothing measurable to the firefight. However, it is the immeasurable aspects of what we do that may be decisive. Unfortunately, there is no way to prove it. Would they have been as confident going down the alley if we had not been there? They know that if push comes to shove we can bring in assets and medical care that they cannot. More importantly, if we had not been there, would the same locals who asked for the shurta's help and later praised them, have assumed that the National Police were militia and accused them of being part of the problem? It happens all the time. So if my team had the same effect as the diploma on a doctor's wall, then so be it. We returned home glad to be back in our relatively quiet neck of the woods.

Two days later an American Apache helicopter watching a gunfight in the same neighborhood mistakenly engaged and destroyed a pickup truck from the first battalion and killed four shurta. Two steps forward one-step back.

Figure 33: 5-2NP Shurta conduct pre-combat inspections prior to a patrol

About two weeks ago, I had an interesting conversation with some Iraqi men down in one of our market places. A few middle-aged men had approached me and were skeptical about the work we were doing. One said he wished that he could trust the Americans, but he just could not bring himself to do so. I asked if things had gotten better since February when we had arrived. He admitted that they had, but reminded me that that was only four months out of four years. I agreed and talked about some of the positive civic improvements that were going on around him. He said he would try to be hopeful, and maybe he could meet me there in a few more months and tell me if his mind had changed. His friend, who had remained silent, broke in and asked, "Why is it that when you invaded Kuwait the country was fixed in just a few months and is now once again very rich and prosperous?" I choked up on my bat, ready to knock this one right out of the park. "Well sir, that is pretty easy. None of the Kuwaitis ever shot at us when we tried to help them. More importantly, they did not waste time attacking each other. Four years later you all can't seem to put your weapons down long enough to build anything!" He was stunned … and silent. A third man, a bit older, had said nothing during the exchange. He put his arm on the second and said something in a low voice. Bahaa was mounting back up so I had to make my apologies and leave before hearing what he said.

Later that afternoon I was sitting with a few of our terps and talking about the second bombing of the Golden Mosque in Samara that had just happened that morning.[13] We were all taking our best guesses on what the Iraqi people's reaction might be. Frank stopped all of a sudden and looked at me. "Sir, do you remember the conversation we had in the market earlier today, about rebuilding Kuwait?"

"Yes" I replied.

"Do you know what the third man said to his friend as we were leaving? He told his friend that you should not ask American officers questions when you know the truth of the answer will break your heart."

---

[13]   The Al-Askari Mosque in Samarra is one of the most important holy places in Shia Islam. It is home to the remains of the 10th and 11th Imams, and is adjacent to the shrine of the 12th Imam, Muhammad al-Mahdi from which the Jesh al-Mahdi draw their name. The golden dome of the Mosque was destroyed on 22 February 2006 and started the wave of ethnic violence that reversed the tide of the war and necessitated "the surge." On 13 June 2007 a second attack destroyed the two remaining minarets and threatened to spark a new wave of ethnic violence just as "the surge" was beginning to show signs of effectiveness in some areas.

Update #18: 4 July 2007—The Shoe Drops

I sat with two other U.S. lieutenant colonels, a major, Staff Sergeant Pettus, and a terp along one side of a very long conference table in a cavernous hall on the second floor of the Iraqi Parliament building. Brigadier General Bahaa and his staff rounded out our team. On the far side of the table, a collection of Iraqi deputy ministers-of-this-or-that waited patiently for the meeting to begin. About eighteen hours prior Brigadier General Bahaa received a summons to meet with one of two Deputy Prime Ministers, Mr. Salam al Zaubai, on the topic of the Haifa Street Project, and to "bring his Americans along with him." The U.S. Brigade commander, Colonel Roberts, was home on leave so our small band was dutifully playing backup to Brigadier General Bahaa in an engagement that was significantly above our pay grade.

The Haifa Street Project is the brainchild of the 2nd Brigade 1st Cavalry Division "Black Jack." In a nutshell, it is an urban renewal project along a three-kilometer stretch of high-rise apartment buildings that cut a swath through the heart of the city's oldest section. Saddam originally built the area in the early eighties. It should be no surprise to anyone that there is a lot of historical tension associated with it. I have described this area several times previously as a cross between Miami and Stalingrad. The project concept is simple. Secure the area. Create as many visible signs of change as possible. Fix the minimum essential services to get people back into the area and then use that momentum to extend out into the surrounding neighborhoods and to push for projects that are more significant. After four months, our efforts are bearing fruit.

I have described many of the initial efforts at securing the area in previous letters. We have been hugely fortunate that the substantial increase of forces in the district made possible by the "surge" had a measurable and, so far, lasting deterrent effect on the enemy. There is more than just anecdotal evidence of Haifa Street terrorists captured in other districts because they were looking for easier places to operate. Sadly, that is not entirely true and every day we face challenges that range from murder to extortion to politically motivated suicide bombings. But all at a level low enough that life has gotten significantly safer for the average resident of our area and both individual and government workers are going about the business of rebuilding.

Many of the schools we visited in February have already undergone the entire process of writing statements of work, bidding for contractors, obtaining funding, and actual construction. I cannot overstate how transforming it is to see two or three freshly renovated schools clad in new bright coats of paint and standing proudly as a centerpiece to a neighborhood. More important is what is going on inside. I have had more than one child tell me how proud he is of his new school and that they look forward to going there again in the fall. Last week the Iraqi school system finished their annual nationwide testing—similar to New York State Regents tests or other ones around the country. Brigadier General Bahaa's men had spent the week guarding the various test sites and ensuring the students safety. In a conversation with the head of the Baghdad testing office, he was proud to learn that in our district over 95% of the eligible students took the test. The only real hic-up in the whole process was a sad bit of business where apparently someone stole the test booklet for the "Islamic Studies" portion of the test. So that had to be moved from the first day of testing to the last. It seems to me that if I were going to steal a state exam, I would go for the Algebra test!

Figure 34: The Haifa Street Project brings life back to this once thriving district

All up and down Haifa Street, small things are being done to make visible changes every day. Local men are on the payroll to continue the enormous trash removal problem. Locally contracted masons rebuild the security walls around apartment complexes and the local soccer field. Old posters and advertisements have been scraped off walls. Curbs have been repaired, trees planted, bullet holes patched, and a fresh coat of paint gives it all a new feel.

For the last few months, the brigade has been installing streetlamps, both solar and conventionally powered ones. Every week the previously haunted streets become more inviting. In our meeting the deputy prime minister made a comment that "terrorism is a darkness, that can't always be fought with a sword or a gun, but must be fought with light." He was almost certainly referring to light as a metaphor for goodness and justice, but the simple fact is that light, or more specifically power, matters! In a country where power almost always requires a gas run generator that means fuel. For all of those pundits who have long been shouting that this war is all about the oil, I say "You're right!" but not for the reasons you think you are.

The enemy is fuel. The black market in fuel is the source of no end of corruption as the Ministry of Oil fails to provide the supply to a subsidized market. Local gang leaders infiltrate the fuel distribution process at every level, taking their cut and financing terror. The average civilian has no recourse. Without fuel for generators, air conditioners, refrigerators, water pumps, sewage pumps, TVs, lights and cell phone chargers all fail. In one hundred and fifteen degree heat life gets miserable fast without some combination of those things. While the Blackjack Brigade is working a variety of creative solutions to solve the generator and fuel distribution problems, Brigadier General Bahaa is focusing his efforts on the area's three gas stations.

I spend far too much time at the gas stations. I vaguely remember watching the news as a young kid and hearing about the gas lines in the 70's era of Jimmy Carter … although strangely I don't ever remember actually sitting in a car waiting in line. Thank you Mom and Dad! However, I get to watch it now with much of our time devoted to trying to design traffic flow that minimizes the potential for car bombs and working to prevent corruption. Sadly, the biggest offenders are the various personal security detachments of government officials who routinely break in line and use their position to get extra fuel while citizens wait. In a country where bribery is the norm a few extra bucks or a relative at the station almost ensures that there are more vehicles in the cut lane than the actual one. We have done some things to prevent that, not the least of which is stationing Brigadier General Bahaa's men to oversee the stations, hoping that we can weed out the corruption in our own easier than we can in others.

Collectively all of the efforts by the U.S. soldiers of the Blackjack Brigade and the Iraqis of Brigadier General Bahaa's 5th "Sword" Brigade have made a serious impact and have drawn some attention. A meeting with the U.S. Ambassador the week before and now the meeting with the Deputy Prime Minister were held specifically to see what the Iraqi government can do to reinforce an essentially grass roots efforts to bring Haifa back from the dead. The meeting went well. Like most Arab meetings, there were not a lot of specifics decided, but it was clear that some government attention was coming our way.

On the wall in front of us at the meeting with the Deputy Prime Minister was an unusual painting. I was attracted to it partly for its style and more than a bit by the vibrant blue and yellow pigments the artist chose. But what really captured me was the content. An angel knelt in prayer. Above the angel's head, in what could loosely be construed as a thought bubble, was a collection of Babylonian style hieroglyphics and images. While I am certain the Muslim artist did not intend it, all I could see was a Christian angel desperately praying for some solution to the disaster in the cradle of civilization. How appropriate that it hangs above the Iraqi decision makers. I am sure it went completely unnoticed by all but me.

After the meeting, our smaller group was invited up to the Deputy Prime Minister's office. It might have been Louis XIV's office for all the ornate furniture and frilly curtains. Mr. Zaubai[14] took the opportunity to give us a bit of his philosophy. Of particular note was a comment he made about America. He said, "Americans are the most generous people in the world. That is because they are still a young people, made up from all over, and they are not burdened by their past wars—they do not carry them around in their hearts. For that reason you can meet an American and become friends with them very quickly." As much as I wanted to enter a debate on that subject, it was not the time or place. However, it seems to me that American's do carry our wars with us in our hearts, certainly our soldier's do. The difference is that our wars have advanced the cause of freedom and we have a tradition of not being beaten. The difference between the American way of war and what the Arabs carry as their burden is that we are gracious winners. We have historically gone back and helped reconstruct those countries we have fought and left them better and freer than we found them. That is difficult for a society of victims to grasp.

My team spent the Fourth of July doing pretty much the same thing we do every day. It would have gone largely unmarked if not for the festive decorations in the mess hall. A hamburger and some potato salad were about the only links to what I would have been doing back at home. At a meeting that afternoon, Brigadier General Bahaa made a point of wishing all the Americans a happy Independence Day. His heartfelt reminder was yet another indication of how much of the rest

---

14   Salam al Zaubai is a prominent Sunni politician. He was wounded in a suicide car bomb attack earlier in March 2007 and treated in American medical facilities.

of the world really does admire us and how much of a struggle remains here for us to finish.

Later that night Bahaa and I found ourselves summoned to a 2100 hours conference at his Corps Headquarters ostensibly on the topic of improving living conditions at some of our checkpoints. Within minutes, I realized something was not quite right. The correct combination of people was not present. While we waited for this meeting to materialize, we drank some chai with the commander of the National Police who had been Bahaa's instructor at the Iraqi War College. Major General Hussein is a tiny little man with bad teeth, a lazy eye, crooked smile and a razor sharp mind. He took us to the officer's mess and back to a borrowed office. For two hours a small collection of us chatted about all things but business. He likes American and British novels and history, so the subjects ranged from the Civil War, to Mark Twain, to the atomic bomb, to Agatha Christie (who lived in Mosul for a while and wrote several novels based in Iraq). It made for an interesting celebration of the Fourth. Eventually the Commander of Baghdad arrived and the shoe finally dropped.

The Prime Minister's office had issued a warrant for Brigadier General Bahaa's arrest.

Update #19: 8 July 2007—The Riot

Needless to say I was a bit stunned by the news. I imagine I felt much like Commissioner Gordon must feel when the Joker drops into his office in a cloud of laughing gas surrounded by hooligans. "Holy sectarian motivated hatchet jobs Batman!"

Lieutenant General Abboud, the commander of all Iraqi Security Forces in Baghdad, is rather large for an Iraqi and his normally humorous eyes are set deep in a walrus-like face. He looked anything but happy. He, Major General Hussein, Brigadier General Bahaa and I went into his office to talk alone, chai being the only interruption. In quiet tones the specifics became clear.

I wrote previously about one of the very earliest operations we did when taking over our current area of responsibility. We had rounded up a bunch of Sunni detainees and ended up releasing ten for lack of evidence. Those released included "the Egyptian" I described back in March. (Sadly, I have not seen him in several months. Hard to say what his fate might be.) This was the incident I wrote about several months later when the intelligence section of the Prime Minister's office interrogated Bahaa. When that brigadier general informed then Colonel Bahaa that the investigation would be "placed in a bottom drawer in case it was needed later," he was not kidding. The ridiculous charges that Brigadier General Bahaa had taken bribes to let Sunni detainees free was surfacing in a politically motivated attack by one of the Prime Minister's underlings to discredit one of the Iraqi security force's fastest rising Sunnis. Apparently, that reality, coupled with the fact that Brigadier General Bahaa's younger brother Colonel Alla just took command of the 6th National Police Brigade, was too much for various Shia factions to stomach.

Lieutenant General Abboud did what he could to calm Bahaa's fears while getting all the facts. While he had Bahaa write down a sworn statement, I gave Lieutenant General Abbud my take on the events and all the reasons why the Coalition Forces and I had not only underwritten but also actively encouraged the release of those detainees—a total lack of evidence being chief among them. The fact that it almost certainly began the process of building some level of trust between that Sunni neighborhood and the largely Shia National Police was another goal, but went unstated in this context. A little after midnight we took our leave with the assurance from both commanders that they would take no action until they had a chance to speak with the Prime Minister personally.

Unlike the good Commissioner Gordon, I do not have a button under my desk triggering the Bat Signal to light up a cloudy night sky. However, I did have email, and given that the night was crystal clear with no clouds to bounce a signal off, it would probably be more effective anyway. Needless to say this particular bit of injustice traveled around Baghdad fast. Maybe not as fast as the fifteen-month extension news of the spring, but damn close. The Coalition began making their case while Lieutenant General Abboud waited for an audience. Bahaa and I continued about our business: another meeting with Dr. Chalabi on Haifa, a command and staff meeting, and a late night patrol … the details of all a bit fuzzy as two nervous days passed with no news.

Figure 35: Unknown officer, Lieutenant General Abboud, Brigadier General Bahaa and Lieutenant Colonel Green at the Baghdad Operations Command Headquarters

Patrolling helps Bahaa relieve stress, so we did just that. We had word that the meeting with Abboud and the Prime Minister was in progress and the suspense was palpable. We headed over to the neighborhood that was at the heart of the controversy. I attempted to give out a box of Rice Krispy treats, but the youngsters refused to get into a line and not push each other. So I put them back in my truck and headed into the alley to catch up with Brigadier General Bahaa. The kids were not pleased. The young man I had enlisted a few weeks back in the bag of trash for a soccer ball project gave me a particularly malevolent glare. I caught up with the boss who was already in conversation with several of the older men. They were concerned that the new electrical wires that had just been installed might get knocked over if one particularly dilapidated old structure fell over. After almost a year without power they were not willing to take any chances now that hope was in sight. Several minutes later the supervisor of the electrical team that was working this part of the project appeared. He eagerly explained to us the progress they had made. They had all of one type of wire installed and were now just waiting on a supply of the second gauge to finish the work. He was on track for a load test in two weeks and if all went well this neighborhood would be one of the first to reconnect to the power grid. He proudly explained that his entire team lived in the neighborhood and that they were in a race with the muhalla to their south to see who could finish first. Given that these two neighborhoods have historically fought with rifles and hand grenades, I took it as a good sign.

On the way out of the alley, I ran into some old friends unexpectedly. Somehow, in all my previous updates I have failed to mention that my old battalion, 1-14CAV "Warhorse" had joined the Blackjack Brigade back in May and was working alongside my National Police unit in the Haifa Street area. This was the unit I fought with in Mosul in 2004 and which I had left reluctantly a year ago when I was assigned to the Transition Team mission. Needless to say it has been hugely comforting to work alongside so many old friends and to watch appreciatively as their professionalism continues to ease my work with the National Police. We took few minutes to chat and to snap a photo of Lieutenant Colonel Jeff Peterson, Brigadier General Bahaa, and myself at the spot that I increasingly see as the benchmark for progress in our district.

Figure 36: Lieutenant Colonel Jeff Peterson, Brigadier General Bahaa, and Lieutenant Colonel Green

An hour later the moon was up and we headed north on the main four lane highway through Karkh. Well past curfew our convoy came to a complete stop. We were near one of the gas stations so I figured Bahaa had spotted something odd. I dismounted and moved forward to greet my brightly smiling friend. "Lieutenant Colonel Green, I have good news! Lieutenant General Abboud just called. He talked to the Prime Minister and they dropped the charges. Bear hugs are hard in full body armor, but the attempt was credible. He grabbed my hand as we started walking and he rattled off his thoughts in the rapid speech I have grown accustomed to when his mind races. He normally spares me the hand holding because he knows it makes Americans uncomfortable. I give him some leeway when he is really happy about something. The team does not bust my balls about it too much anymore. I have seen at least a few of them trapped into a bit of hand holding embarrassment with one of their counterparts. One of these days I am going to jog by the General after a successful mission, slap him on the ass and yell "good game!" just to see his reaction to a peculiar American habit.

The next day we celebrated by going to the zoo. Well, sort of. What we were really doing was going to provide a bit of extra security and mingle at the "job fair" being conducted in one of the parks in the zoo complex. For several months now the brigade's civil affairs folks have been working with the local district government to establish a chamber of commerce and tackle the unemployment problem. It is no easy task. The chamber of commerce was a difficult concept to get them to buy into. We originally had the fair scheduled almost a month ago, but curfews imposed in the aftermath of the second Golden Mosque bombing in Samara had forced us to postpone it. Twenty-four local companies and four international companies had all agreed to set up booths and take applications. An entry survey would help the chamber see what kind of skill sets and demographics were represented amongst the unemployed.

We showed up at the main gate of the zoo about half an hour before the event was supposed to start. The crowd was forming fast and was contained in the parking lot waiting for opening time. The actual fair site was about five hundred meters away and out of sight. The relatively calm nature of the crowd probably lulled us into a false sense of security as the shurta began to take up positions next to the private security forces belonging to the zoo. About five hundred males crowded behind jersey barriers to the left and about fifty young women lined up orderly to the right. It is customary to form two lines. As the published start time approached, we prepared to search individuals before they entered, suicide vests being the worry of the day.

As the clock ticked forward to 0930 an evil spirit descended upon the male crowd and the relatively orderly group panicked. While the females proceeded in order through the line and had their bags checked the men all surged forward pinning the mass against concrete barriers and crushing people as they tried to squeeze through the openings to get searched. They immediately began to spill over the barriers. General Bahaa's men moved forward and began shouting. The mob had no ears. The General surged forward arms spread and pushed the tide back over the wall. His men followed, fortunately all keeping their weapons lowered and under control. A momentary pause gave us time to think. I stepped forward next to one of the entryways: Captain Ly at one flank and Frank the terp at the other. Major Brede and Doc took the other entrance. In the time it took to regain some order with the men, fifty women were all searched and on their way. We slowly started getting the men through. Each was convinced that if he were not first then there would be no job. There was no way to convince them that the companies were just taking applications today.

In a relatively short time, the first group of five hundred was in and the steady, slow flow of additional applicants was easily withinin the capability of a few guards. We estimate about 1500 arrived over the course of the day. We started moving down to the job fair site. As we crested the hill and approached a high arched bridge over the man-made lake we saw our next challenge. The leaders of the pack had all arrived at the reception tents of the fair and were filling out applications. The fastest were complete and in line at the lakeside pavilion which had previously been an upscale restaurant. It now housed the prospective employers. It was obvious to the organizers that they already had more folks than they had anticipated and someone had decided that they would block off the bridge and regulate the number actually in the tent area at a time. The zoo security guards were desperately trying to stem the flow as we arrived. The only other Americans were all down at the restaurant building and too far away to help.

As we stepped up onto the bridge from behind the crowd, things got ugly. The crowd started heckling the guards prompting one to plant the butt of his AK-47 squarely into a young agitator's face. As

I strode forward, the crowd surged on him. In the press, the guard's rifle discharged and the tight mass of bodies flew apart with a handful of men all clutching various body parts. Unharmed myself, it took only seconds to scan the scene and determine that there was no blood. The bullet had mercifully fired straight down into the concrete and, while several received blows from flying cement fragments, fear was the worst of the damage for all but the one young man with a bleeding but unbroken nose.

Bahaa barked a command and his shurta surged forward seizing the five zoo security guards and confiscating the weapons. The crowd, momentarily stunned by the noise and violence, was temporarily relieved of it's unemployment induced panic. The shurta relieved the guards of their weapons and cleared them to prevent further accident. Placing the guards in flex cuffs drew a cheer from the crowd. There are very few forms of life lower in many Iraqis' eyes than the National Police and the private security guards are among of them.[15] A bit of a shouting match between Bahaa and the head of zoo security followed, much to the delight of the crowd. My teammates walked the leading edge of the mob silencing the hecklers by staring them down. We called our trucks forward to give us some more deterrence and for the next hour or so were relatively successful at keeping the crowd calm and metering traffic into the event.

Bahaa and I went down to speak with the organizers leaving Major Brede and crew up at the bridge to do the work. It is good to be king. Things inside were going well. The District Area Council members and chamber of commerce representatives were delighted and the employers all steadily went about their business. The citizens, after filling out an application and no longer suffering from panic

---

[15]   The Ministry of the Interior maintained a wide range of police forces to include: The National Police, Traffic Police, Patrol Police, River Police, Border Police, and Highway Police. In addition Most of the Ministries maintained a wide variety of security guards for fixed site security. "The Surge" placed the District Commander in command of all security forces in his district. Making that plan a reality would consume much of Brigadier General Bahaa's time and energy. We never made as much progress in that regard as we should have, but it is one of the things I believe brought us significant success.

were all smiles. Everything was on the up and up—until we went back outside.

Back by the tents the organizer in charge of handing out the applications had reached for the final stack in his box. The crowd having realized that there were more people than visible applications panicked for a third time. The organizer, who had a well-developed fight or flight instinct, chose the latter and made a straight line for the first American he saw. He handed the stack of papers to Major Koast, my team's military policeman and the only one of us with any formal riot control training. As I stepped out of the pavilion, Scott clutched applications in one hand and his pistol in the other, shouting at the top of his lungs while he moved back toward the trucks. Doc and Sergeant First Class Babb raced towards him from that side while Major Weiss, Captain Lee, Bahaa and I moved in from ours. Forcing people to sit down had proven to be the only useful technique of the day and within a few minutes we had everyone back on the ground long enough to find another case of applications.

When the box finally arrived they began to rise at once and lurch forward. Weapons raised, we got them to subside. At one point I yelled something to the effect of "Are you all a herd of animals, or are you people?" Before my terp could repeat it, one twenty-something young man looked at me, raised an eyebrow and in a tentative questioning English voice replied, "We're people?" I broke out laughing. I turned to Bahaa who was now personally handling the applications, grabbed one and handed it to the young man. "People indeed, good luck with a job." Somehow we were able to get an application into everyone else's hands without further incident. The organizers fed us lunch.

As we were wrapping things up a young man on a bike sped over the bridge and apparently took the turn too tight and did a header into the asphalt. He approached us bleeding from a severe gash in his head. Doc went to work gleefully. He loves stitching people up and quickly had a great big needle of anesthetic loaded causing a significantly unhappy look on the victim's face and jeers from all his friends who found the show hugely amusing. Most of them calmed down when Doc brought out the stitching needle, morbidly fascinated as the stitches went in.

Meanwhile, one of my new terps was playing at a different kind of doctor. Sam is our newest addition. In his mid twenties, Sam is an

Iraqi Christian with a large build, light hair, and light complexion. We tease him that he really must be Canadian. Almost invariably, when he is wearing American ACUs, the locals fail to recognize he is a terp until he opens his mouth. One of the booths inside the fair belonged to the international company that manages all our interpreters. Two young Iraqi women, probably deliberately picked for their attractiveness, ran the booth that day. Sam had his eyes on one and quickly found out that neither of them had a ride back into the Green Zone. As it happened we had two spare seats in the Hummers and that was our destination. Bahaa, overhearing the conversation, sealed the deal and before I knew it, my terp population had temporarily doubled. Sam got a phone number. The team spared him the embarrassment of a standing ovation only because we did not think of it in time.

It seems Bahaa is right; the Baghdad Zoo is for lovers.

Update #20: 20 July 2007—The CASH

"Six, this is five, ya see the smoke?"

"Roger, looks like it's in our sector."

"Check it out?"

"Please."

We turned right, back into the heat instead of left and back home. An afternoon meeting and lunch with a panel of retired four-star generals making their rounds at the beck and call of some congressional or presidential commission had gone exceptionally well. Nothing else was on the schedule and the previous few days had been hectic so we were going to pack it in early. Unfortunately, a tall pillar of black smoke was a very clear indication that the plan was changing.

We had not heard the explosion earlier. Acoustics in the city continue to baffle me. Some of the largest booms go completely unnoticed, yet a distant boom will roll me out of bed over the sound of both air conditioning and headphones. Without having heard it, the visual signs brought the event together quickly. A car bomb had detonated just off the side of a main road and had ignited four or five cars adjacent to it. The cluster still burned intensely while a crowd of Iraqi Police looked on. National Police shurta, from one of our subordinate battalions scurried around trying to restore some order. Several hundred meters down the road it looked like one of their

143

trucks was shredded. We pulled up as close as seemed prudent and dismounted.

Sam and I waded into a crowd of locals and Iraqi Police asking questions as we went. As the story started taking shape an American platoon arrived to help secure the area followed shortly by Iraqi fire trucks. The well-practiced crew doused the raging fuel fire in white foam leaving the charred automotive remains in a drenched cluster. The car bomb had detonated as a National Police convoy had passed by on the way to deliver dinner to one of the checkpoints. The fire had been raging for somewhere between twenty to ninety minutes depending on whom you asked. Iraqis are hopeless at telling time. I suspect it was closer to twenty as my team was the first on the scene and the road is heavily trafficked by military convoys.

Determining the casualty count was equally frustrating. The wounded had already been thrown into the back of National Police trucks along with the dead. The whole lot were evacuated hastily to a nearby hospital. As the numbers sorted out it looked like one National Policeman killed with nine others wounded. The residents suffered as well with another Iraqi national killed and four of them wounded. As the cars became safe to approach we were relieved to find that no one had burned to death inside—a small mercy. While my dismount team asked questions the vehicle crews passed the appropriate reports and got in touch with Bahaa. He would be out shortly.

Bahaa was not going to be happy. A chain and bollard fence blocks the side road to through traffic. That allows the neighborhood to limit entry to a few checkpoints and provides an increased sense of security to the residents. However, it has the unfortunate side effect of creating a small parking area. This area, together with a variety of others in the neighborhood's busy market district, has long been a concern because they provide a tempting target for car bombs. The General has been working diligently with the neighborhood councils and local police to prevent residents from parking in these most dangerous areas, but has met with less than satisfactory results. The paradox of improved security is an increasing unwillingness on the part of the population to follow the precautions that allowed things to get better. Today it was clear that the local police's inability to enforce the no parking rules had terrible consequences.

While I mused on Bahaa's likely response the National Policeman on the scene continued to try and keep curious onlookers away. They were pretty hyped up having just evacuated so many casualties, but the major in charge was doing a credible job of keeping order. Then things went to shit.

Across the divided highway from where I watched, and on the other side of the now smoldering cars, was a small row of businesses, all with their security fences lowered but windows shattered from both concussion and shrapnel. A pair of shurta kept onlookers at bay. One, I would learn later, took his rifle and knocked out a piece of broken glass from one of the storefronts. Hard to say why he did it … frustration, anger, ill intent. Regardless, the populace always assumes the worst about the police, and immediately stirred into motion. A Sudanese man watching from and adjacent courtyard emerged and made a beeline to the store. Confronted by the police, he began a shouting match. I have no idea what he said, but the previously efficient major began beating him. Within seconds others emerged from the courtyard and the shurta closed into a tight knot. Rifle butts and batons emerged.

"Doc, Koast, on me!" They had been looking the other way, but quickly understood. They and Sam joined me in the sprint across the burning wreckage and into the crowd. In those few seconds an old, black burqa clad woman and several more men had joined the fray. The Iraqi major was steadily smacking the crowd down. We each grabbed a shurta and flung them from the group. Our sudden appearance was surprising enough to get all parties to separate and desist. The major did not need a terp to understand my command for him to get back to his truck. All was quiet for the few seconds it took everyone to catch their breath. Then the verbal assault on Sam started as an ever-increasing crowd tried to talk all at once. I try never to show anger when talking to the locals, but they were trying my patience. Eventually I pried the fight participants from all the extraneous witnesses and started hanging facts on the skeleton story I had observed.

The Sudanese family lived adjacent to a string of money exchanges. The first man from the courtyard works for the owner as the security guard. When he saw the young shurta break the glass he assumed it was an attempt to use the explosion as an opportunity to loot the money exchange. I have no idea what he said to the major, but given his agitated state I am certain it was confrontational. Iraqis are outrageously vocal in their disrespect of all civil servants. On the other hand, I have little doubt that the Shia major was eager to beat down a foreign, and almost certainly Sunni, outsider who was blatantly challenging his authority at the scene of an explosion. The Sudanese man could very well have been the triggerman, given the location of both his house and shop.

While I gathered up what appeared to be the local leaders and lectured them all on the need to work with the police and not deliberately provoke them, Bahaa arrived and waded into the Iraqi security forces with every bit of the fury I had expected. Gathering up both the National Police major, and the local Iraqi Police captain responsible for the area, a loud and public tongue-lashing ensued on their failure to do their duty and prevent cars from parking in the area. The major, who at this point was not thinking anything through, bowed up and argued back. Bahaa skipped his notorious finger-waving rebuke and escalated straight to an arrest order, sending the major in disgrace back to the trucks. The captain, with more sense, took his medicine. Having watched him vent his initial frustration I walked over and caught him up on what had happened. The situation was largely under control. All we really had to do was wait on EOD to show up and reduce an orphan explosive that had blown clear and lay in the median; a few cracked 60mm mortar rounds that had not gone off in the main blast.

Within minutes Mr. Jammal, the head of our district's Ammanant (public works organization) arrived. A small, penguin like man always immaculately dressed, he is a constant feature amongst the people of our district. Much like Bahaa, he is always out and about and is a bit of a media whore, often taking credit for projects initiated by Coalition forces. In spite of that, he is one of the few who legitimately seems to working for the good of the people and is part of the solution. His team of workers immediately began sweeping the streets and removing the signs of violence. Getting the area quickly back to normal is an important part of the process. While the sweepers cleaned, the Sudanese family brought out water jugs for Bahaa's policemen. The difference in manners between the shurta my team works directly with and that of other units is often night and day. With any luck our actions mitigated the previous abuses to some degree.

The EOD team arrived after almost an hour. A young sergeant declared that this was "his" incident scene and began barking orders. That kind of statement is almost deliberately calculated to piss me off and was not well received by Bahaa either. Our work largely complete and the threat of half a mortar round being relatively insignificant, I decided it was time to go. "Saydee, let's go to the hospital and check on your shurta ... they don't need us here." He jumped into my HMMWV. His trucks scrambled to mount up and followed us south.

Figure 37: VBIED in the Kindi Neighborhood

We pushed our trucks into the crowded entry of the hospital. Sam, Doc and I trailed in Bahaa's wake as we pushed into the emergency room surrounded by a swarm of Bahaa's personal security detachment. It was complete bedlam and the introduction of another fifteen did nothing to help. National Policemen from the unit that was hit crowded the waiting area while their wounded comrades were being worked on inside. There was no method to the madness. As we worked our way in a gurney was working its way out. Bahaa pushed passed to start asking questions. I backed out to keep from being part of the problem.

Inside the emergency room a tall Iraqi Lieutenant Colonel saw me and frantically pushed through the crowd toward me. In perfect

English he introduced himself as Lieutenant Colonel Fahil, the Ministry of Defense liaison to the hospital and told me that the man they had just wheeled out on the gurney was a shurta injured in the car bomb. His femur was crushed and the injury was well beyond what the local facilities could handle. The bleeding was too much. They were loading him up into the ambulance to take him to the best hospital in Baghdad, but that was at least a forty-minute ride and at this time of day probably twice that.

"Doc, Sam, go find out what you need from the doctor. Lieutenant Colonel Fahil, we will take him to the CASH[16] in the Green Zone. Is he in the ambulance now? Tell the drivers to follow the second HMMWV. Bahaa! Mount up, were taking this one!" I vaguely heard the Lieutenant Colonel's thanks, but the relief in his eyes was obvious. We burst back out into the afternoon heat. This was turning into a long day. Major Brede was on the ground outside the truck. "Were heading to the CASH! That ambulance is coming with us. Doc has the report; get him on the medevac net. Bahaa, come with me. Have your guys wait at the bridge." The seven-kilometer race began.

The trip did not take long, but seemed agonizingly slow; every speed bump fraying the nerves. Entry control points, designed to save lives, now frustratingly delayed our attempts to save one. We made radio contact with the CASH so they were expecting us. The team helped transfer the patient to a small ATV for movement into the emergency room, an American medic taking over from the Iraqi ambulance crew. Bahaa, Doc and I shed our gear and a medic escorted us inside while the team parked the vehicles nearby. Our walk was largely silent. A few quick questions as we went inside linked us up with the right set of staff. We found seats in the corner. I consumed a bottle of water in seconds. Bahaa declined and paced, as anxious as I have ever seen him. At the reception counter the staff chatted quietly and joked and talked happily about whatever kept them going from day to day while the young shurta lay inside. I clenched my fist knowing that they saw this every day; it was part of their world. I had no right to judge.

---

16   The Combat Support Hospital or CASH is a military hospital that is deployed forward into theater. It is larger than its more famous cousin, the MASH-mobile army surgical hospital.

Minutes later a tall doctor emerged; he tossed blood stained gloves into a waste can and approached me. He determined I was who he was looking for. "The patient arrived with no pulse. We conducted a scan to determine if there was any brain activity to attempt resuscitation. He was dead before he got here." He turned and walked away. That was it. Nothing else. Indifference. Just one more dead Iraqi. I should have punched that fucker.

Doc coordinated getting the shurta's remains out to the ambulance so we could take him home. Bahaa and I walked slowly out to the trucks. Soldiers know when not to talk and when questions with one word answers are the best defense against public tears.

"Saydee, do you know his name?"

"Not yet ..."

The team waited in the shade of the large trees that make the Green Zone green. My crews mingled with the civilian ambulance drivers and the cousin of the young man who had, until a few minutes before, been struggling for life. Our premature return announced the unhappy outcome without need for the confirmation we eventually voiced. Failure is an emotion that mixes poorly with grief.

Later that night, at various times and each in their own way, all three of the interpreters that were there that day found me. The conversations were all eerily familiar.

"Sir, I wanted to thank you for taking that Iraqi to the CASH."

"Of course, why wouldn't I have?"

"Well, he is Iraqi; you didn't have to do that."

"He was human, of course we did."

Update #21: 31 July 2007—Miss November

Bullets snapped through the trees overhead. We quickened our pace. The staccato of gunfire had steadily increased for several minutes and showed no signs of abating any time soon. We ducked into the safety of the palace rather than continue the trek back to our trailers. PT gear is no great defense against gunfire. We had timed this one badly, forgetting completely as we emerged from the mess hall that the Asian Cup championship game would end at almost exactly six-thirty, barring any tie.

I had witnessed the full fury of celebratory gunfire during the Olympics in 2004, the night sky awash with the light of tracers and flares. No such visual pleasure this year, just the auditory certainty that what goes up must come down. It is a somewhat disturbing state of affairs that in the six months we have been here not a single American has been wounded by hostile fire in our area of operations. Yet each of the two final soccer matches produced a casualty due to lead rain. Last week one of the lieutenants working in the brigade was hit in the head by a falling round. Fortunately, it just grazed him. Sergeant First Class Sartin saw him in the laundry the other afternoon apparently getting ready to go on leave. The bullet remains in his scalp waiting for removal back in the states. I doubt he will ever shed the obvious nickname, "Bullet Head," with which he was greeted by the troops. Minutes after

151

I left the chow hall, a bullet penetrated the ceiling and struck a young female soldier in the shoulder. A surreal event described by the team members still sitting nearby. She too will be fine, but probably without a cool new moniker.

Injuries and deaths occurred all across the country in the bizarre expression of national patriotism and joy. Our terp Frank's brother was wounded in the leg. In his case, the perpetrators may have actually been using the confusion to shoot people deliberately. An American sniper shot one of the two gunmen involved in that incident. All of the individual pain and suffering aside, the Iraqis are universally ecstatic over the win and in the early hours of victory attribute to it a great healing quality. We shall see.

I, for one, fail to see soccer's allure. The following day every channel showed the clip of the only goal scored … over and over and over again. While I generally shared the pride our Iraqis felt in their team, I couldn't help but give Brigadier General Bahaa and his staff officers a hard time. They really need to find a sport than can generate more than five seconds of highlights and thirty minutes of celebratory gunfire.

Sports seem to be increasingly on the Iraqis' minds. This weekend saw the first annual Karkh District swim meet. Planned entirely by the District Advisory Council, Iraqi security forces planned to provide additional security for the event and to attend the awards ceremony. I had to witness this! I find it hugely ironic that after six months of making the district safe enough for the Council to sponsor community events they would use their newfound freedom to jump deliberately into the Tigris River for a swimming race. In the words of one skeptical trooper, "The real race is which contestant will die of disease first."

We were all running late on the day of the event. Blackjack Six (the U.S. Brigade commander), Warhorse Six, Brigadier General Bahaa and I linked up on the ground right as the event was supposed to start. Unfortunately, the race's planners had given us some bad information about the location and there were no swimmers in evidence. While a battery of cell phones was called in to work the problem one of the young soldiers commented, "Just look for the ESPN 8 film crew; they have to be covering this important event!"

We eventually found the correct location, a large floating barge jutting out from the bank several kilometers down stream from where we were told to go. We arrived just in time to see roughly fifty swimmers slipping out of the water and into the festive atmosphere of one of the river's "casinos." The tent covering the volleyball court sized barge provided a welcome relief from the blistering sun. We pushed our way past the cheerful crowd on the bank and into the awards ceremony. Local government officials and civic leaders sat on the couches in the front row with a throng of onlookers and competitors crowding in behind. Bahaa and Blackjack Six are both local celebrities and were warmly welcomed, giving speeches and eventually awarding prizes.

When the contestants all started moving up toward the awards stand the barge started listing noticeably. There was no apparent danger until one exceptionally large council representative, affectionately referred to as Pac Man due to his perfectly round physique, began moving toward the front. I took the opportunity to reposition myself back by the gangplank. I have seen enough redneck home videos to know how this one played out. My team still reminds me consistently of the folly of my Tigris riverboat cruise several months back and I was not about to give them further ammunition.

The ceremony complete, the delegates began withdrawing from the tent. I had met most of them previously, but one in particular caught my eye. A very young religious Imam, immaculately clad in rich traditional garb and flanked by a half dozen very attentive aides and a pair of police officers. My terp whispered the Imam's name in my ear, saying that he was one of the famous religious leaders of the neighborhood. He could not have been more than eighteen years old. Nevertheless, in a culture that passes religious leadership down by the generation, they held him in significant reverence. I had to shake my head. At age eighteen the only religious experience I can recall was sneaking a peek at Miss November at the newsstand. I cannot possibly imagine what this young man had to offer anyone in terms of religious insight. Maybe that is part of the problem.

Back safely on land we took the opportunity to walk a stretch of Haifa Street. It was now early evening and the hundred and twenty-degree heat was easing up as the sun's direct rays fell behind the high-rise apartments. We strolled past newly painted kiosks, repaired curbs, and through renovated playgrounds. We stopped in a local pool hall and chatted up the locals. What was an empty lifeless urban canyon back in February is now once again a vibrant community. It is by no means complete. It still requires military checkpoints. Many of the apartments are still empty and in need of renovation. Power is still intermittent and water not always reliable. There are still nefarious characters looking for the opportunity to do harm. However, the sense of terror is largely gone.[17] In January, this area averaged six dead bodies a day. It is unusual for us to have six in a month now. It is hard to tell how long it will take this fragile equilibrium to develop deep enough roots to be sustainable over the long term. The consequences of underestimating would certainly be brutal

I wished our guests were still with us. Earlier in the day the Brigade had hosted William Kristol of *The Weekly Standard* fame and historians Fred and Kim Kagan. Brigadier General Bahaa hosted them for lunch the previous day and early in the afternoon, the U.S. and Iraqi command groups had the opportunity to take them for a mounted tour of the Haifa area complete with a walking tour of the now flourishing Al-Alawi Market and one of the Haifa Street apartment complexes. While the atmosphere at the peak of the day's heat was overwhelmingly positive compared to their similar visit back in early May, the evenings are really the best opportunity to take the district's pulse.

I will be anxious to see what items from the visit make it into the news. I hope that it reflects the sacrifices of both the Iraqi and U.S. forces that have toiled for the last six months and are justifiably proud of the measurable success we have achieved. I have generally taken a dim view of the Fourth Estate, but am encouraged to see them arriving in country in increasing numbers to see it all first hand before passing judgment in September. I was encouraged to see an op-ed article in the *New York Times* the other day entitled "A war we just might win." Given the traditional stance of both the authors and the publication, it was a refreshingly candid confirmation that someone other than the military is actually paying attention to the impact the surge is having across Iraq.

I hope that Congress will stop taking political advice from twenty-something interns resulting in the embarrassing congressional slumber

---

17   The violence in these neighborhoods had stopped being characterized by Sunni vs. Shia gangs. It was replaced by a growing power struggle of rival Shia Jesh al-Mahdi factions trying to gain control of local resources such as fuel, kerosene, and alcohol.

party held last week and pay more attention to what is going on outside the beltway. They should consider taking a harder look at what the world needs outside of the context of the self-interest generated by the 2008 campaign. Here is an idea. Why don't we bring all those young interns to Baghdad and introduce them to that silly young Imam and his friends. Maybe we can change some Iraqi hearts and American minds. And Mom, for the record … the Miss November thing was a joke.

Update #22: 10 August 2007—The March

The rhythm of the rotor blades picked up speed and the bird's weight shifted slightly followed by the magical moment when the connection to mother earth is broken and flight begins. Brigadier General Bahaa grinned from ear to ear. A fighter pilot in his youth he has had only a few opportunities to fly since the Iraqi Air Force ceased to exist back in 1991. A few years back, when working as an election official out in Anbar, he had ridden in a Chinook, but this would be his first trip in a Blackhawk. His son Mustafa sat next to him: it would be his first flight ever. Momentary weightlessness in the surge of takeoff took Mustafa by surprise. Two hands began clutching at his father's leg. Bahaa put a gentle hand over the boy's to calm him.

Mustafa, a slight seventeen year old who is apparently an accomplished violinist but can no longer attend music school, is Bahaa's youngest and, not surprisingly, spoiled child. While not officially a shurta he nevertheless wears a National Police uniform, carries a rifle and patrols regularly as part of his father's personal security detachment. It is not an arrangement of which my team and I are particularly fond. The lad has a tendency to wear his father's rank and to come and go, participating as he pleases. Bahaa feels he can best protect him by keeping him close, so I grin and bear it.

The pair of Blackhawks quickly gained altitude and raced off to the south then banked hard over the river giving us a bird's eye view of Baghdad's primary oil refinery and power plant. Unlike my previous trips over the city it was early morning and I was not buried under a mound of my own equipment. The view revealed the landmarks of the city all around us. Every detail familiar, garnered from countless hours spent pouring over satellite imagery and maps and patrolling the streets. We skimmed over rooftops and headed back north, our quarry finally in sight. Tens of thousands of Shia pilgrims swarmed out of the slums of Sadr City and the muhallas of East Baghdad and were funneling onto two narrow bridges on the their way the Kadhimiya Shrine to the north.

The day's march, in memory of the death of the 7th Imam Musa Al-Kadhim, had been our concern for several weeks. The Iraqi military chain of command was taking security very seriously. Two years ago the threat of a suicide vest on one of the bridges had caused a stampede, breaking the guardrails and killing almost a thousand as they tumbled into the Tigris. With all the recent sectarian violence and the politics of the summer on everyone's mind, today's event had the potential for disaster. The Iraqi army and police had done a total recall of all forces from leave, boosting available manpower considerably. A vehicle curfew reduced the significant threat of car bombs. Nevertheless, in the end, several million Shia were going to march right through the heart of historically Sunni areas and it was anyone's guess what the day would bring.

Our day started early. By six in the morning we linked up with the General at his headquarters. A quick cup of chai and we were on our way. We had a few hours before we needed to link up with Blackjack Six at the helipad, so we headed along one of two march routes to the southern bridge. At six there had been only a handful of marchers in small knots. By seven there were large groups organized into "parades" and chanting under various leaders. We fought our way to the bridge. By seven-thirty the main four lane arteries of our district were pulsing with a constant stream of marchers. We pulled over at the bridge and dismounted, my team and Bahaa's Personal Security Detachment struggling to maintain a protective bubble as we moved against the flow and up onto the bridge. Bahaa's battalions protected both ends of the bridge and we moved to inspect them.

The morning had dawned blessedly cool for August. The temperatures had been dropping steadily from a high of about 125 degrees a few weeks earlier to just over a hundred that morning. The marchers were fresh, most having emerged from the neighborhoods closest to the river. Full of energy, they repeated a single chant over and over. The sight of Americans prompted each passing group to new levels of enthusiasm as if in attempt to convert or provoke us. Doc, Sergeant First Class Babb, Captain Roedick, Tony and I trailed along in Bahaa's wake largely ignoring the challenge. Bahaa set a quick pace as we cut through the sea of marchers and a quicker one on the way back as we flowed with the tide. Having tasted what the day had in store for us we mounted up and eased out of the crowd on our way back to the waiting birds. Major Brede and Colonel Mohammed would take our patrol out while Bahaa, Mustafa and I went joyriding.

Well, maybe I should say while Bahaa and I went joyriding. For Mustafa there was little joy. As we banked hard again and raced down Haifa Street, with high-rise apartments at eye level, Mustafa lost his battle with motion. The contents of a near empty stomach fought their way up in dry heaves. Blackjack Six fished around in his kit bag and handed our young hero a beef jerky pouch against any further emergency. Much to the amusement of the Americans present, Mustafa spent the rest of the trip staring unhappily into a plastic bag, the smell of teriyaki almost certainly doing nothing to alleviate either his nausea or his embarrassment.

Figure 38: Mustafa enjoys his first helicopter ride

The rest of us focused on the view. By nine in the morning all three of the major entrances into our sector were flooded. The mob steadily poured out the two main exits to the shrine several miles to our north. Security checkpoints, patrols, and sniper positions provided a blanket of deterrence, but no iron-clad guarantee against misfortune. Pilgrims marched past the zoo or over the bridges past the train station and the airfield, or up Haifa Street. Local civic organizations dotted the route with sanctioned tents providing limited food, shade and refreshment. It was inadequate. There were no latrines anywhere. Some questions are best left unasked.

By ten in the morning we were back in the trucks. Mustafa curled up in the back seat of our trail HMMWV and passed out. Bahaa mounted up in his up-armored Silverado and led us into the eye of the storm. Our trucks plowed through the masses making only marginally better time than the mob around us. Flags waved, marchers sang, young and old, women and children. The bright greens and yellows of Islamic banners contrasted sharply with the black of the women's burqas and the all too frequent black of the Mahdi militiamen who crowded the ranks. The same chant echoed over and over. "Allah is great, blah, blah, blah … death to our enemies" with fingers pointing to us, or fists beating on chests.

As we pressed north the crowd grew increasingly hostile. Given the time and distance involved, this group would almost certainly be those who had emptied from Sadr City at first light, those most opposed to us. The percentage of young men was significantly higher than at other times of the day. Emboldened by the mob surrounding them and the heady enthusiasm that ritual chanting evokes in the mindless, they looked for ways to act out defiance. The chants became more frequent and spitting on our trucks was a favorite sport. The most defiant employed the ultimate insult, taking off a shoe and throwing it at us. Shoes began collecting on the top of our Hummers. At day's end we had at least one matching pair, one on my truck, and one on our trail vehicle. I cannot help but think we got the last laugh. The shrine was still several miles away and the asphalt was getting hotter and hotter as the noontime sun found its full fury.

Bahaa's shurta were taking their share of abuse as well. I suspect much of it suffered because we were with them even if the General would never tell me so. Up ahead sudden movement caught our eyes. A surge of bodies raced toward a center point. A rifle crack! We pushed forward; the shurta began surging out of open truck beds to push back the crowd that surged forward to see what had happened. The tide momentarily stemmed and I dismounted with Doc and Sergeant First Class Babb flanking. A lowered shoulder or two into an encroaching crowd provided breathing space. Bahaa and his officers waded into the fray, separating the crowd from a pair of visibly distraught young shurta who he sent back to the trucks. Apparently, the verbal abuse had become too much for some of the young men in the lead trucks and a scuffle ensued. Age and wisdom prevailed over youth and passion, as the two sides separated. We mounted up and headed south. Nothing good could come from provoking the mob further.

Figure 39: Shia Pilgrims flood across the bridges over the Tigris and into Karkh during the 7th Imam Pilgrimage

We paralleled the railroad and much to our surprise, a four or five car train passed us pulling south. The Baghdad train station lies unused most days. Open briefly in 2004, the number of attacks made it impossible to sustain its use. Today however the old green cars were pushing north and south, packed to overflowing. The roofs were crowded with exuberant young riders; it was a disaster waiting to happen. Safety, I am certain, has no direct translation in Arabic. Several hours later we would learn that one Iraqi died and seven more wounded due to electrocution aboard one of the trains. I was not surprised.

Back down south we made the jump from the western route over to Haifa Street. This was our turf. We were playing at our home stadium now and the crowd was much different. The locals at the side of the road all knew us and the pilgrims coming in over the northern bridge were not as likely to be from the most extreme Shia neighborhoods. The crowds still chanted, but much of the anger was missing. We dismounted and walked another kilometer of the route this time without incident. We mounted up and drove back south through one of the adjacent Sunni neighborhoods. They quietly went about their business in small coffee shops and pool halls staying mostly out of sight and keeping the kids off the streets.

Back in the traffic circle at the northern bridge we parked and set up camp. Blackjack Six had joined us on the ground and we expected Bahaa's Iraqi commanders to join us soon. It was now close to 2p.m. and the tide of people still flowed steadily over the bridge from east to west and making its turn north. The first tenuous ebb of visitors started making their way backwards against the masses. It was getting hot. After almost seven hours I climbed in the truck for a break. Sergeant First Class Carrejo snapped a hasty photo as proof that I succumbed to a short nap.

By fifteen hundred the tide had reversed with the vast majority of marchers now on the weary return trip. A handful of National Police vehicles, ambulances and a lone bus made an all but futile attempt at shuttling people south. We watched incredulously as each successive trip managed to pack more and more people into each vehicle. The arrival of each ignited weary marchers into a frenzy of activity as they raced, trampled, pushed, shoved and beat each other, oblivious to age or gender, to find some hand or foothold. It was shameless.

An old man dropped to the ground in the intersection: clearly the heat had taken him. The shurta dragged him to the side of the square and into the shade. My docs went to work. I had brought extra medics with me today. Sergeant Novatny was back with us, having grudgingly returned to his unit when our own Staff Sergeant Ethington had returned from leave. Captain Roedick, one of the brigade's physician assistants, joined the team for the day's event against any unforeseen tragedy. We also had two new terps. Rafid was back after having left us for a job with the Ministry of Oil in March. He was not making enough to support his pregnant wife. We suspect he just missed us too much to stay away. Tony had joined us about a week earlier. He has been terping for almost four years now. Both would perform flawlessly and with great compassion over the next several hours. A bag of I-

V fluids fixed the first grateful old man. According to the old fellow Captain Roedick's efforts had earned him a "castle in heaven."

Figure 40: Captain Roedick leads the effort to treat heat casualties during the 7th Imam march on Haifa Street

Within an hour we had established a full-up casualty collection point, and all three docs were fully engaged. The tide was now in full flow back south. The day's heat had peaked and whatever meager water the event's civilian organizers had given out had long since been consumed. The crowd's enthusiasm for chanting had largely faded with their thirst. Exhausted masses trudged south. The women, wrapped from head to toe in black and often far too large and out of shape to be marching any distance, bore the brunt of the sun's punishment. The crows started falling on our curbside as if plucked from the sky. The docs went to work administering I-Vs and pain medication while the rest of us secured the area and vetted the crowd for those with the worst symptoms of dehydration. We had brought enough water to do some good and pulled the worst to the side and distributed what we could. One obese old crow glowed red and by the dryness of her face had stopped sweating. I asked Staff Sergeant Pettus to get a bottle of water from the cooler and get it to her. He raced off and caught up with her handing her the bottle. She took it gladly, until she turned around and focused long enough to see that an American had given it. She gave it back.

Others in equal peril were far more willing and grateful for assistance. We treated fifteen or so with I-Vs, and dozens more with liquids. I have very little doubt that at least four of them would not have survived the journey home had we not intervened. As my team labored away Bahaa's men provided security and managed the increasingly hectic flow of transportation. The worst of the heat victims were pulled over to the side and eventually moved onto women only busloads. Obnoxious males were forcibly removed to allow patients into the vehicles. The selfishness of the average Iraqi was extraordinary as was the courage and patience of Bahaa's men. It is far too easy for us to judge the Iraqi security forces, and they are far from our own soldier's standards, but they are hard young men who increasingly stand out for their sacrifices and devotion especially when juxtaposed with the rabble of the slums.

Another organized parade passed and spotted us treating our growing mass of patients. The parade leader fired up the chant "Allah, blah, blah, death to our enemies" waving fists in our direction. One of the men sitting on our curb resting joined in the chant. Our terp Tony became irate and laid into him. "I have been riding with these American's all day today. For almost twelve hours they have listened to Muslims wish death upon them. They have been spit on, they have been degraded, and they have had shoes thrown at them. Yet here they are at our parade, treating our sick and giving you water to drink. Do you see a single Shia doctor helping anyone? Were any Muslims giving out water? And all you can do is chant stupid slogans." Tony vocalized in a few short sentences the heart of the problem and the truth stunned the man.

Today was a holy day for Islam; a day that inspired an expected three to five million people to walk dozens of miles to honor a fallen Imam. For weeks I have been asking my various Iraqi friends to explain the event to me. What is its' religious significance? Why is it important? The answer is wholly unsatisfying. We are marching because he was the 7th Imam. Well, what did he do? None of them could tell me. He did not appear to have achieved any great purpose, no societal or religious reforms. From what I can tell the only things that he appears to have done are father the 8th Imam and die. Inasmuch as it takes no particular skill to have achieved either of those unremarkable tasks, I left wondering what the day was about. I had hoped having watched it I might learn. Maybe the march would be filled with joyous songs that would bring about a sense of community, charity or some other praiseworthy value. Ultimately, the only consistent attributes I witnessed were selfishness as they fought over limited resources and anger as the end of every religious utterance called for the death of those who were not like them.

Tony may not have specifically recognized it, but what he saw in the Americans is the legacy of our largely Christian heritage: turning the other cheek, the Good Samaritan, loving thy enemy as thyself, doing unto others. The values of our nation's historically dominant Christian faith express themselves daily in the actions of our soldiers. Those in uniform represent a wide range of faiths and a widely divergent degree of commitment to them. What is so obvious to me, time and again, is that even those who do not maintain a deep personal faith still demonstrate the best social aspects of it. This war may look like many things from the outside looking in. On the ground, in the filth of the street, in the heat of the day, in the throng of the crowd, it is about good and evil. Allah may be great, but it is often a U.S. Soldier armed with American values and an I-V that fends off death.

Figure 41: Nazeh Samer Salh "Tony" at the 5-2NP HQ

Figure 42: Khalid Khudeir Khalil "Al" at FOB Proseperity

Figure 43: Asaad Foud Abd El Salam "Asaad" at Muthana Airfield

Update #23: 19 August 2007— Frustration

Some days it is hard to tell if things change around me or if it is me who changes. The night is blessedly cool. The sun's brutal rays are no longer able to sustain the grueling pace they set in July. Darkness brings welcome relief and soldiers start emerging from their climate controlled boxes for reasons other than work or survival. A cigar smoker stares absently into the palm trees. A reader struggles to focus in the dim porch light of his hooch. The soft notes of someone learning to play the guitar echo from down the row. Doors once again crack open letting light stream out. Small groups talk quietly. The temperature today is exactly the same as it was when it first pushed us all indoors several months ago. Only our perception of it has changed.

So much of what we do here has become very commonplace after eight months. Arabic no longer sounds odd to me. I rarely notice the calls to prayer. I notice when a street is unusually clean, not when it overflows with trash. Nothing that a child does in the street strikes me as dangerous any more. Everywhere we go we meet people we have met before. There seems to be very little new and the days start blurring together. Every now and again, something particularly absurd stands out.

◆　　◆　　◆

A few weeks ago Brigadier General Bahaa and I received a call to a late night meeting in the palace. The exact same sort of unexpected meeting that almost landed Bahaa in the hoosegow. (My grandfather always used to say hoosegow. I have never had the chance to use it in a sentence and this seems as good a time as any ... but I digress.) So we went to the meeting on a topic I can no longer recall. As we left we were called to the side and told that a target on the wanted list had been spotted and we were tasked to go seize him.[18]

Several hours later we found ourselves in an old government compound that was abandoned but now houses a small population of squatters. The night was overcast with a moon that occasionally broke brightly through the clouds. Otherwise it was painfully dark. This was not one of the areas blessed with any power, and the squatters were far below the income level that makes generators possible. We had already cleared the first apartment, locating the target's brother and wife and obtaining leads to a second building. My tolerance for uncertainty lowers significantly the farther I get from the original information I am given. Bahaa was quickly leading us to the end of my patience.

His men flowed into the subsequent building like water into a maze; not what I had hoped to see. I kept my team close. We moved into the foyer and guarded the escape route and lower hallways while listening for the sounds of progress above.

Staff Sergeant Pettus, Doc, Rafid, a few shurta and I scanned the room under-gun lights cut bright swaths before our night vision goggles. The place was a shambles but there was no obvious threat. We waited while Bahaa and crew worked upstairs. Doc called out to the trucks to let them know where we were. Minutes ticked by. I glanced in his direction ... and froze. I knew I was not seeing what I thought I was seeing. There, on a bookshelf, not a foot from Doc's head was a huge rooster—sound asleep. I broke out laughing and the obvious bawdy jokes raced through my mind. Doc raised a quizzical eyebrow "what?" A shurta flooded Doc in the beam of his flashlight. Staff Sergeant Pettus, seeing what I saw, joined in my mirth. Doc turned

---

18   This cell was a Jesh al-Mahdi mortar cell that had been conducting attacks into the Green Zone. We were starting to notice a growing trend of the Shia dominated government targeting Shia militia groups, especially when the attacks were directly against the government.

and looked past it at first, focusing just in time to see a shurta poke the sleeping bird sending it into a panic-induced dance around the room and down the hall. That night we captured two targets suspected of sectarian killings, but we failed to detain the cock.

◆   ◆   ◆

On a sweltering afternoon several weeks later we conducted a similar raid in one of the older neighborhoods and came up empty handed. As we wound our way out of the warren of small alleys, stepping over streams of sewage and ducking under low hanging wires, General Bahaa stopped short at a familiar house, and said, "I want to introduce you to someone." His guys spread out in the ally and he knocked on the door frame and called softly inside. A quick conversation and he was invited inside waving me in after. We ducked past the curtain that served as a door and down a short hall into a courtyard of sorts.

The courtyard was roughly fifteen feet on a side with an ancient wooden balcony providing a mere semblance of a roof around the edges. Another ten feet up, what should have been a roof had long since collapsed. Now nothing blocked the sun. Around the open room was a smattering of furniture. An old wooden couch contrasted sharply with a very new looking refrigerator idle due to a lack of power. A stove, a table, a few chairs, not much more. I took it all in quickly as Bahaa explained. "I come here to visit the old woman, who lives here, she is very sick." Indeed she was. The small creature occupied a tiny fraction of the couch that filled the corner with the largest portion of overhead cover. She wheezed audibly. Two other women and a handful of kids stood nearby. Bahaa introduced us.

The youngest of them was in her early forties and relatively attractive. I suspect that is how Bahaa met the grandmother, but it was not the time to ask. She spoke passable English and insisted that I sit down on the couch next to the matriarch. With a sheepish smile she apologized for not having anything cold for me to drink. I cannot imagine feeling more out of place. This kind of poverty is shocking every time I witness it. I was at a loss for words. Kids are always a good place to start. Grandmothers all love to talk about grandchildren. Bahaa and the younger woman translated.

I quickly learned that granny had lived in the same house since 1939. All of her male relatives were dead. She was being supported now by her daughter and granddaughter and enjoying her great grandchildren. A framed family portrait on the wall, showing a clan of probably fifty, hinted at the potential magnitude of her lifetime's worth of loss. I shared a picture of my girls with her. She kissed it, saying how much she knew I miss them. I imagine she does. I wanted so very badly to do something for this family. They had almost nothing. I asked if there was anything they really needed that I might be able to find. From under her robes the old woman pulled out a small purple plastic box. She opened it up and revealed a blood sugar testing kit with an inoperative battery . I looked up past the useless refrigerator and out the open ceiling, a tear forming. Dear God, where am I going to find one of those?

◆   ◆   ◆

The great dream of almost every terp is to obtain a visa to the United States. Much like Willy Wonka's golden ticket, it dominates their thoughts. This provides no end of entertainment as my team administers various American trivia tests to see if they are fit for admittance into the country. Rafid is the preferred victim in this sport. Asked to name five American Presidents, he responded, "Bush, Clinton and Lynn Colin."

"Lynn Colin?" we asked. "Do you mean Lynn Cheney ... or Colin Powell?"

"No!" he replied. "Stop messing with me, Lynn Colin ... he freed the slaves!"

Game over. He is now one of us. I know I have seen that on Jay Leno before.

◆   ◆   ◆

A few months ago I wrote about a meeting with one of the Deputy Prime Ministers of Iraq. At that meeting, one of his assistants handed out business cards to those present. Most Iraqi officials have dual sided business cards, one side in Arabic and the other in English. I flipped his over to see what his duty description was. "Assistant to the Deputy

Prime Minister for Entertainment and Trysts." Hmmm, I bet I could get his terp a slot on David Letterman. Sounded like a great job to all of us!

Figure 44: VBIED at the Yarmook gas station ignited a fuel truck and kills fifty men, women and children

A small white piece of paper flutters in the breeze pulling against the tape that holds it to the wall. On it, the photocopied face of a young girl smiles. Graceful Arabic script portraying the heartbreaking message: Have you seen this child?

We have been at this wall many times over the last few months. It marks the boundary between the road and the fuel station. A few weeks ago we could go nowhere near it … the fire was too intense. A car bomb had detonated. The explosion ignited a large fuel truck that in turn engulfed the crowd of men, women and children waiting to buy fuel for their homes. The walking wounded, almost forty, had already been evacuated when we arrived. The dead and dying lay beyond help. The tanker threatened to explode at any minute potentially igniting the nearby underground tanks. The Iraqi fire department showed up shortly thereafter, and for the next thirty minutes did nothing short of heroic work in quenching the flames. The damage was mind numbing. We watched helplessly as fifty-two victims were pulled from the debris. The child's body had not been identified among them.

Major Tom Weiss, one of the officers we work with closely had been with us at the gas station several days prior to the bombing. He takes many pictures. Scanning through them he stopped short. There, on the computer was a picture of the same girl and her mother, standing in line holding a gas can. She was the same age as my daughter Alexandria and had the same dark brown eyes …

It is a damn good thing we get to laugh occasionally and that, some nights, the heat feels cold.

Update #24: 7 September 2007— Enough

I sat in the back corner and finished a silent prayer. I quietly surveyed the room while those who surrounded me finished their own. We sat in a small Huseniya, an Islamic place of worship, more like a community center than a true Mosque. The room was quiet, filled with mourners. They say that bad things come in threes ... maybe because that is when humans say to themselves, "enough is enough," and we have to package things together to prepare ourselves for the next set of three.

Lieutenant General Abboud, the impressive Iraqi Corps commander who informed Brigadier General Bahaa of his arrest and eventually fought it off, sat near the entrance. I had never seen him in civilian clothes: his suit was tailored expertly. However, he looked small and fragile. The death of his mother two days prior had obviously hit him hard. He looked very tired. We sat quietly. My Iraqi friends know I am curious and they could see me focusing in on various aspects of the room. Colonel Mohammad explained a basket of hockey puck size objects in the corner. They were small clay disks stamped with a picture of the shrines at Karbala and made from mud taken from that area. Shia, who commemorate the battle of Karbala, place them on the carpet in front of them as they pray. Bahaa caught me eyeballing a series of strings running diagonally across the room atop the Persian rugs at one meter intervals—they mark the direction to Mecca and line up worshipers and ensure they are evenly spaced and don't knock each other over as they execute their prayers. I was more than familiar with other aspects; the inevitable Chai and Turkish coffee providing welcome points of familiarity.

This was the third wake in as many days. One of Brigadier General Bahaa's subordinate battalion commanders had lost his father a few days prior and, most tragically for us, General Bahaa's mother had lost her fight with breast cancer late last week. In Arab culture the family sets up a tent or a gathering place and for three days family and friends come to pay their respects. It was more than a bit humbling to see the genuine regard and respect that the community felt as the greater Baghdad civilian, military and tribal communities came and went. It left Bahaa exhausted and without any time to grieve. I am not quite sure how he managed.

I am glad that I had gotten the opportunity to meet her. On that one occasion she and Bahaa's wife explained to me the secret of Iraqi chai, which, for those who are curious, is not at all like the crap you get at Starbucks. The secret is a clove like seed called "Hell" which apparently comes from India. Mixed with the finely ground tea leaves, both are steeped loosely in boiling water. The slight spice of the Hell cuts the bitterness of the tea and a healthy dose of sugar seals the deal. While certainly not a family recipe, I will probably always think of it that way.

Fortunately, all three deaths were of natural causes, an odd sense of normality in a world that is otherwise far from normal.

It has been awhile since I have written, not so much because there has been nothing to write about, indeed in some regards the pace has accelerated, but more because I find it increasingly difficult to put things into context. The last few weeks have just felt odd. Like there is something big just ready to happen and, if I wait another day, the story will write itself. Then I wake up and it is three days later, but the other shoe still has not dropped.

I imagine much of that feeling comes from the insanely artificial deadline of September 15th and the much-anticipated report to Congress. It is the elephant in the room that no one will acknowledge. Except that we all do. Visits by famous media personalities, politicians and pundits hit a feverish pace over the last few weeks. For the first time in a long time I actually look forward to reading the news and seeing articles with some meat on the bones and written by someone who at least saw it all first hand. I will paste in the text of an article written by Ralph Peters, a somewhat controversial commentator, with whom I often, but not always agree. Because his article describes many of the places and people I have introduced you to, I think it will provide a useful contrast.

New York Post
BACK FROM HELL
By RALPH PETERS

August 31, 2007 -- AO WARHORSE, IRAQ

IF you saw any news clips of intense combat last January, you were probably watching the fighting unfolding on Baghdad's Haifa Street: 10 days of grim sectarian violence.

Until we put a stop to it.

The boulevard of Sunni-inhabited high-rise apartments erupted in shootouts pitting the "Haifa Street Gang" and its al Qaeda allies against heavily Shia Iraqi army units. It was a recipe for massacre, as terrified residents - those who remained - cowered in their apartments.

Then the U.S. Army moved in. Commanders must've felt tempted to just level the former Saddamist stronghold. Instead, they decided to rescue what they could. Our troops cleaned out the terrorists with what Brig. Gen. Vince Brooks - one of the Army's rising stars - termed "very focused kinetic effects."

And the Cavalry charged in: the 2nd Infantry Division's 1-14 Cav, OPCON - Army-speak for "on loan" - to the 1st Cavalry Division's 2nd Brigade.

This is a ride-to-the-rescue outfit in the old Cavalry tradition. Shifted from one hot spot to another in their wheeled Strykers, 1-14 Cav has fought its way through the streets of one gut-shot Iraqi city after another.

BUT Baghdad was the big one. Not only because it's the capital but also because our changing strategy suddenly opened new opportunities to reset the terms of our presence.

Initially, Haifa Street was a brawl-for-all. Even now, the troopers of 1-14 Cav keep their "sabers" ready. But a patrol through the sector on Tuesday evening revealed changes many the media just won't credit. (We're not supposed to win, you understand.)

Six months ago, terror ruled. The streets were empty of civilians. Shops were shuttered, facades were shot up, and hate graffiti covered the intact walls. Power was out, and the district was out of hope. The residents who could leave had already left.

It would've been easy to write off Haifa Street.

Instead, 1-14 Cav and their foster parent, the 2nd brigade, 1st Cavalry Division, switched gears. First, they won the fight. Next, they were determined to win the peace.

AND the numbers in "AO Warhorse," their area of operations, reveal an impressive transition from a hellhole to a livable - if still understandably nervous - neighborhood: From 74 attacks on our troops in January, the violence dropped to 20 attempts in August. And they were minor attacks, compared to those of the past.

Overall, murder rates in Baghdad are down by two-thirds, while attacks on the Iraqi police and civilians have declined for months. In fact, 2nd Brigade is now "out of the checkpoint business," according to its commander, Col. Bryan Roberts. With the Iraqi police doing its job, Roberts can muster as many as 34 combat patrols a day - the presence we always needed and didn't have.

And plans are already in the works to turn the district over to the Iraqis.

During the mounted segment of the patrol, I asked Gen. Brooks - who stood tall in a Stryker's hatch beside me - if he worried about a surge in al Qaeda incidents in the remaining weeks before Gen. David Petraeus reports to Congress.

Brooks realizes how badly the terrorists yearn to embarrass us, handing ammunition to the just-quit camp. But he told me we'd just broken a key al Qaeda network that was planning dramatic eve-of-testimony strikes. Other terrorists might still manage to stage attacks, but the organization's spinal column was broken.

MEANWHILE, our "urban renewal" of Haifa Street became an accelerating success. En route to Combat Outpost Remagen, we saw people of all ages in the streets, a half-dozen soccer games under way, patched and repainted facades - and even new solar street lamps (a big hit in a power-strapped city).

It was all part of an innovative small-is-beautiful approach to gaining trust and helping Iraqis get back on their own feet. The administration's initial policy of funding huge projects to be developed by multitentacled U.S. contractors failed miserably. But our soldiers are making progress where favored contractors only ripped off the taxpayer for billions.

How? As Col. Roberts put it, "Micro-everything is good." Our troopers have backed micro-projects, such as community generators, awarded micro-grants to jump-start street-level commerce, and favored a ground-up version of capitalism, rather than the administration's dysfunctional marriage of profits at home and socialism in Iraq.

The Iraqis get their batteries charged. Once. Then it's up to them to make their neighborhood - and their country - work. Lt. Col. Jeff Peterson, 1-14's commander, adds that the "spontaneous economic development" that followed the establishment of security and face-to-face engagement with the population has been inspiring.

It is. As we dismounted from our Stryker to walk the streets and alleys, Sunni residents - once hostile to Americans - crowded around to thank our local commanders, all of whom were well known down in the 'hood.

OF course, other sectors in Baghdad remain contentious, and progress can be reversed in the wake of a single trigger event.

But even across the river in Rustamiyah, where the troopers of the 1st of the 8th Cav - a butt-kickin' outfit - have been fighting Muqtada al Sadr's Mahdi Army in urban-guerrilla warfare, hopeful signs are emerging. A few days ago, Mookie unilaterally announced a six-month timeout for his gunmen. Partly, it's a political move - but it's also due to the sacrifices and fortitude of 1-8 Cav and other frontline units.

So why don't you hear more about our military's successes? It goes beyond the old media dictum that "if it bleeds, it leads." Plenty of journalists have staked their reps on our predicted failure in Iraq - and they hate the reversal of fortune the surge is achieving.

God knows plenty of problems remain. Iraq's government isn't much help - none, as far as Haifa Street's revival is concerned. And five minutes away, there's a bustling Shia neighborhood. Not long ago, the residents were all Sunnis. Shias with a new-born sense of entitlement (and a vicious militia) drove them out.

Nor have all of those who used to live on Haifa Street returned - they're being coaxed back bit by bit.

But those familiar with the desolation-row atmosphere that prevailed just months ago are encouraged by the progress. Iraqis have begun to help themselves, while their government squabbles.

AFTER winding our way through a lively market, we stopped by a riverside cafe. Its patio was crowded in the softening evening.

The establishment had been reopened with a grant of pennies from the Cav and 2nd Brigade. At the sight of us, the owner rushed to tell everyone that we would always be welcome as his guests. He was excited about the future - almost to the point of weeping.

Outside, in the orange twilight, 1-14 Cav's Maj. Dave Stroupe and I paused on the embankment above the river. A micro-grant had cleared away years of garbage. Kids were swimming, while their elders fished.

Every so often, a corpse still floats by. And the mahalla, or neighborhood, across the river is still seeded with terrorists. But the precious normalcy around us represented a true and wonderfully human victory.

Smiling at the hubbub on the cafe patio and the laughter from the kids splashing in the shallows, Maj. Shoupe shook his head in wonder.

"When we came down here in January," he told me, "the only people we saw in the streets were shooting at us."

Then the U.S. Cavalry rode to the rescue.

Sadly, I did not get a chance to meet Mr. Peters again or introduce him to Brigadier General Bahaa or the many other brave Iraqis who have had no small part in the success in our area. As much as we can all be proud of what American forces have achieved in our district over the last few months, the only measure of success that matters is if Brigadier General Bahaa and men like him can carry on when we leave.

That really is the fundamental question of September, and one that is almost impossible to know how to answer. When have you done enough? When have you made enough money to retire? When have you taught your children enough values to let them loose in the world? When have you stored enough grain for the winter? When have you done enough to ensure victory?

I do not think any of the Union generals on the long march back from Gettysburg, told *Harper's Weekly* that was the turning point of the war. Yet today few will argue that the first few days of July 1863 and the victories at Gettysburg and Vicksburg spelled defeat for the Confederacy. Two years later men were still giving their lives to finish the work. In towns like Bastogne and on ships out at Midway, the average twenty-year old soldier or seaman almost certainly had no idea that the corner in Europe or the Pacific had been turned. It all still seemed pretty damn cold and lonely and dangerous to them. However, the simple fact is that the corner had been turned. Sadly, great sacrifices remained.

None of us is going to read anything spectacular on September 15th. Chances are a celebrity scandal or a major storm front will provide the more intriguing headlines of the day. For most of us the day will pass unremarkably and we will go about life normally; attending a funeral, drinking chai with a friend, fretting about our children. The war will continue and, over time, it will become clearer if we have had the defining battle of the war. My sense is that we are in it now, and winning. However, there is no way to know.

Update #25: 23 September 2007— Turning the Corner

We made the left hand turn down by the cemetery and started winding our way into the back roads. As we turned we could see a large crowd forming several hundred meters past the Iraqi Army checkpoint at the corner. The sun was down and what might have given us cause for concern in the spring seemed natural in the fall and even more so during Ramadan when the community gathers in the evening to break their fast and celebrate. Back in the neighborhood, we stop to investigate a set of parked fuel tankers; one empty, and one full. The owner provides some fishy paperwork. The truck does not have proper government markings so we detain the man for questioning and confiscate the truck. An hour later we approach the crowd again, this time coming from the north. I am not surprised to see Brigadier General Bahaa's brake lights glow read. We dismount.

The gathering of males of all ages is festive and they greet us warmly with some chanting. Bahaa in full politician mode grins from ear to ear and wades into the mix, man-kissing the elders on each cheek. I catch up and get sucked into the crowd. Several days before the General had told me about a traditional game called Mahebes or "rings" that occurs during Ramadan. We had apparently just stumbled upon a match of rings and he was eager to show it to me in action.

Rings is a team game, with each family or neighborhood fielding a group of about twenty led by a team leader. Each team gathers on either side of the throng, standing or sitting on low benches or plastic chairs in no particular order. Age apparently is no factor. The leader of the team is armed with a blanket and a ring. He goes to each member of the group, placing the blanket over his head and engages in a conversation and motions that may or may not result in that individual receiving the ring to be hidden in either of his two fists. Once every member has been visited, the team is ready to defend. Twenty poker faces all stand ready to fool the opposing team's leader. The opposing team, having watched patiently, now puts forward their guesser who makes an elaborate show of strolling through the other team observing their behavior—tapping out those he believes do not have the ring. Culling the crowd takes only minutes on this night, but apparently it is not uncommon for staring matches to last for half an hour or more in some of the more ancient rivalries.

Finally, there are just two remaining; the guesser, usually an old and wizened veteran of the game, and whoever it is he has singled out as the guilty owner of the ring. All that is left is to pick the hand. Over the last few days I have had several conversations with Iraqis who have mentioned the ring game and invariably the name of a man called Jasim Al Aswad or "The Black Jasim" comes up. He lives in a neighborhood to our north. Apparently this man's power of observation is legendary and he has led his neighborhood to multiple championships. Tonight age and wisdom overcame youth. The guesser correctly picked the owner but failed to pick the correct hand. His team scores one point, but not the extra. The teams switch sides and start again as we head back to the trucks to mount up. Back on our intercoms, we decide rings would make a great drinking game, an idea certainly not in line with the notions of Ramadan.

Much as the true meaning of Christmas is often lost in the trappings of the season, I can't help but think that Ramadan suffers from much the same problem in its observance. In a nutshell, Muslims should refrain from doing anything sinful (which apparently translates as fun) while the sun is above the horizon. So ... no eating, smoking, swearing, sex, water etc. The notable exception to the exclusion list is sleep, which is about the only redeeming quality of the whole month in my opinion. Having spent the day in misery, the evenings become festive and in general are a time of increased communion with the neighborhood. For those who practice, it is a good excuse to slow the pace of work down during the day. Kind of like a month-long company picnic. Apparently, a few extra prayers are added each day. At the risk of sounding cynical, I cannot help but wonder if those are largely spent asking for the day to be over quicker so they can quench their thirst in the ridiculous heat. Fortunately, the weather is cooling off now and Ramadan, which is on a lunar calendar, did not happen to fall in the height of summer this year.

I have a new favorite Iraqi food, a dish called Moqloba or "Upside-down". Brigadier General Bahaa's wife cooked it for me a few months back, and I suspect that because of my positive reaction, it has found its way more frequently into the rotation. A layer of pulled chicken is spread in the bottom of a medium size pot, probably with some cooking oil. Over that is a layer of sliced eggplant, and then a layer of sliced potatoes about a quarter of an inch thick. The rest of the pot is filled with rice seasoned with some sort of tomato-based flavoring that makes it red like Mexican rice. At any rate, the whole thing is baked and, when ready to serve, is brought out and the pan is turned upside-down onto a large silver tray. Having molded to the shape of the pot, the entire dish looks like a large freestanding rice cake with chicken icing. Mercifully, this is eaten with a spoon and not the goat-grab style free-for-all common for some dishes.

Several blocks further south we stop again. We are back at a familiar corner and I take a moment to speak with a shop owner – the man who angrily showed me the can of food pierced by a sniper's bullet back in February. I asked if he remembered that conversation. He did. "You don't seem as angry as you did back then?" He smiled, "No, I can sleep at night now and not worry." Another elder approached and told us about the power lines that have been going up all over the neighborhood. The work is nearly complete with all but the final connection back into the national grid done. He mentioned that this neighborhood had lost its power just before Ramadan last year and they had all hoped to have it back before the end of Ramadan this year. That was a promise I could not make, but again his tone had none of the anger of the spring, but rather the excitement of someone about to achieve a long awaited goal. I desperately hope to see the project complete before the end of my watch.

Figure 45: Inside the courtyard of a primary school in the Holland
apartment complex - the centerpiece of the Haifa Street Project

Further south, amongst the high-rise apartments, we stop again.
Lately, Brigadier General Bahaa has been confiscating jerry cans of fuel
from black marketeers and redistributing the illegal product to mosques
and needy families in a modern day Robin Hood campaign. This,
coupled with pressure on the sector's gas stations to end corruption
and Coalition efforts to improve the traffic patterns around the gas
stations, has dramatically dropped wait time for legal fuel and dropped

the price of black market fuel. The mood on Haifa Street is light. It is starting to get late, so many of the families have gone inside, but the young men are still out. Six months ago you did not see any young men at all. Bahaa decides to make a game of distributing fuel. Approaching one gaggle of about fifteen high school age kids, he proclaims that whoever answers some Ramadan Trivia correctly will win a can. The first question, "how many verses are in the first book of the Koran?" stumps the crowd. Finally, the youngest of the lot ventures a guess and wins the prize. We move on to an older group, university age guys. After three or four religious questions they give up. Bahaa gives them a second chance and asks a soccer question. To my surprise, they miss that as well. One of their friends approached to see what was going on. Dressed in a *Metalica* T-shirt and armed with a beat up six string, he could have been plucked from any street in America. He begins to make a credible attempt at the opening bars of *"Hotel California."* Bahaa looks at me for approval. I figure I would much rather have the kid memorizing the Eagles than being brainwashed in some Wahabi Madrassa. I nod—fuel for all my friends.

Back into the night, we head into our most dangerous sector. For the last few months, the 1-1-6 Battalion of the Iraqi Army and Warhorse, now replaced by the 4th Squadron, 2nd Armored Cavalry Regiment based in Germany, have been busy trying to end the tyranny of a local Jesh Al Mahdi affiliated gang leader who has dominated the area. A series of raids and arrests has decimated his gang, but the gang's prince has continued to avoid capture and has moved to another district.[19] As we patrol, locals approach us openly with information. Much of it we already know, but their willingness to talk publicly in front of neighbors is a good indication that the fear he exerted may

---

[19]   Hussein Hanni led the Jesh Al-Mahdi cells in the Haifa Street area for most of our time in the district. As the Blackjack Brigade and Brigadier General Bahaa's forces began to have visible progress in his sector, Hussein Hanni fell out of favor with the JAM leadership, and was eventually relieved of his position. He nevertheless commanded significant influence from his time fighting the Haifa Street Gang the year prior, and continued to operate a rogue JAM cell with increasingly diminishing effect. This rift would eventually provide the information we needed to defeat his organization.

finally be broken. One more chapter I hope to see closed before I return home.

Every success seems marred by a setback. A few weeks ago I read an article buried on the back page of the news and deep in the internet about Yarmook Hospital, one of the three main hospitals in our sector. Essentially the article talked about how the morgue, filled past capacity last winter, is now largely empty and the doctors are no longer flooded with violence based emergency room cases. Regrettably, this barometer of success was overshadowed by the Blackwater fiasco[20] which happened just up the street and whose victims ended up in Yarmook.

The Blackwater firefight took place on our western boundary, in the traffic circle I wrote about many months ago where a car bomb had collapsed an underground tunnel screwing up the traffic patterns in the area—the same corner that the crazy lady calls home. The city officials have done great work over the intervening months and have completely rebuilt the tunnel and used the opportunity to overhaul the median and adjacent parks with brick sidewalks and refurbished gardens. The tunnel was set to open again in a few days, but construction equipment still snarled up traffic.

I was not at the scene of the event, but Brigadier General Bahaa arrived shortly after and the video footage his shurta shot of the aftermath and the testimony from people I have come to trust provided me pretty much everything I needed to know. That, coupled with my own observations of the Blackwater employees' arrogance and their outdated convoy practices leave me very little doubt that the incident certainly involved excessive force and was almost certainly avoidable.

I have always held a low regard for mercenaries and have found it more than a bit distasteful that we resorted to their use in Iraq. I have nothing against the huge variety of contractors providing a wide range of support activities. However, the use of violence should be reserved solely to the State. Subcontracting the use of deadly force to those whose motivation is corporate profit and the adrenaline junkies

---

[20]   On 22 September 2007, a patrol from the Blackwater security company killed 17 Iraqi civilians in Nisour Square. The FBI report issued in October found the killings to be unjustified. The incident caused both the Iraqi and U.S. Government to relook the rules and legal procedures governing the use of private security contractors.

they hire is a slippery slope regardless of the previous pedigree of the employees. A security firm has no vested interest in the war being over and no incentive for its' employees to take any risks at de-escalating rules of engagement based on changing conditions in the field. Blackwater is not responsible for interacting with the populace they disrupt and has no need to take risks when they interact with them. My team and thousands of soldiers still serving at wages far below our skills (and far lower than the mercenaries of Blackwater) have all learned better. There are times when assuming a bit of risk brings an overall higher level of security and the economic and political benefits that flow from it.

The single greatest tragedy of the Blackwater incident will be the same as the Abu Ghraib scandal. It will take the focus away from what the Iraq government should be doing to fix itself and allow them to point a finger of righteous indignation st Americans—with much of their population jumping on the bandwagon. This distraction will absorb a huge amount of organizational energy from the Iraqi government in a time when we should be ruthlessly holding them to standards and cutting out the corruption that stifles the growth essential to our success and eventual withdrawal. I hope I am wrong.

Figure 46: Tunnel under the traffic circle several weeks before the
Blackwater incident

Update #26: 22 October 2007— Home

From the cove on the far right bank an early morning mist rolled out, discharging small clouds which drifted across my front in a seemingly endless armada. The first tenuous glow of dawn illuminated their sails as they passed victoriously - as if on parade. The lake, almost perfectly calm, reflected the autumn colors of the trees on the far bank. Below me the gentle creaking of the dock on its moorings provided the morning's only sound.

To the left, hugging the friendly shore, a much smaller squadron of ducks rounded the cape, a pair of fast frigates out front scouting for danger in the van of another dozen trailing in their gentle wake. Low calls signaled a change of course and these newcomers put out to sea, choosing a tack, which would take them headlong into the foggy flotilla and away from whatever danger they sensed in me.

A noisy crash broke the morning calm as a large fish broke the surface and splashed back underneath. Neither duck nor cloud seemed alarmed by the submariner. I jumped. A blue heron swooped in low over the deck, nature's radar alerting him to the aquatic prey. He was silent, but his allies in the trees behind me were beginning their morning pre-flight rituals and the day was soon filled with the strains of nature's song.

The sun, having finally gained some altitude, poured forth an army of rays over the far ridgeline and through the forest leaves. They beat back the shadows in a relentless assault and drove the morning mist back into port. Sun and lake conspired unerringly and illuminated a path to my footstep, reflecting all of God's glory. I was home, safe at my parent's house and, in that moment, everything seemed possible.

By nightfall that illusion had vanished and the struggle between good and evil, joy and pain, sickness and health had reasserted itself and crashed in around me. Having earned a few weeks reprieve from a war now far away, I would face a more personal one at home. My marriage of nearly seventeen years had been failing for many months, and now the tenuous truce was broken. News that my wife had petitioned the court for a temporary restraining order arrived. My plans to return home, visit with my young daughters and salvage what I could were shattered. I bled.

So I traveled and found respite in the homes and company of friends and relatives across the nation. Quiet conversations over a dizzying array of food and more than a few handcrafted ales ensued. Inevitably, the question would arise. Are we winning? Is it worth the cost? I told many stories, but am not sure if the answers I gave satisfied anyone, let alone me.

In a headquarters back at Fort Lewis, I mingled with brothers in arms. Troopers of the Warhorse Squadron, now several months removed from the trials on Haifa Street, were sorting out their futures but eager for news from a conflict in which they gave and achieved so much. Later that night I took much comfort watching these warriors now reunited with their families. Both husbands and wives enjoyed hard won victories over years of separation.

In the quiet suburban home of a friend in Olympia, I met the most charming, fairy-like child I could imagine. Her face lit up as we met and she chattered away a mile a minute, as if we had been friends forever. She has prayed for me every night for the last ten months. I cannot imagine a more powerful force in the world.

In a law office in Tacoma, my lawyer, her paralegal and her assistant worked diligently on my behalf. It was completely unremarkable that I was the only male visible in the bustling office. The fact that it was unremarkable lies in stark contrast to much of the world that still languishes in the darkness and intolerance of cultures and religions that fail to embrace all of humanity's vast potential. I take much comfort in knowing that my daughters will know no such constraints.

In a fast food restaurant in the Salt Lake City Airport a teenage girl asked innocently, "are we still fighting over there?" I could not help but laugh. "Yes dear, we are. And I would most definitely like fries with that!"

At a high school football game in Leavenworth, Kansas, I sat with friends watching their son perform in the middle school band. Last time I blinked, he was a baby. Around me young men and women put the final changes on their early education and were blissfully unaware of how carefree they are, and how their peers in foreign lands are often locked in struggles and violence that are all too real.

At an Irish festival in a small town in Missouri six friends reunited over a few beers for the first time in almost ten years. All of our lives have changed, but we are all exactly the same.

In a sports bar a young college kid took a seat next to me. Thinking he had found a receptive ear, he launched into a bigoted tirade filled with grand proclamations about "bombing them all" and "no ten of them are worth one of us." I took a deep breath. "Son, I have spent a lifetime defending your right to say that, but I don't intend to spend another minute listening to it. Should I leave or are you going to?" He moved to the other end of the bar and watched the game silently. I do not ever recall calling anyone "son" before. I am getting old.

On a sprawling farm in Gregory, South Dakota, my father and I spent a few days in the rain hunting pheasant. The owners, Eddie and Alice shared their American dream with us. Hard work, home cooking and American generosity—a much needed respite from far away troubles.

Over pheasant and wine, the other hunters, businessmen from all over the country, talked about their latest projects and dreams. Never, in a dozen conversations, did the war impinge upon their plans. No factories needed retooling to churn out tanks or planes. No luxury lines needed to be shut down for want of precious resources diverted elsewhere. No shortage of investment capital or real estate. No workers diverted to support a draft. No sign whatsoever of a nation at war.

At a real estate office in Weston, Missouri, I placed a bid on a great little place, looking forward to a new year and a new start. At no point during the process did I answer questions about my race, religion or beliefs. It simply did not matter what neighborhood I chose. I was American and belonged.

At a church retreat near Kansas City, I sat with my Mom at a chili cook-off and pie auction organized to raise funds to support the retreat center and day camp for the urban poor. One more reminder of our nation's desire to do good for those in need and the importance of our faith based values. Mom bid on a pie, to be baked at a later date by a local woman with quite a culinary reputation. She will have to struggle to do better than Mom does.

In countless conversations, individual Americans who understand and are appreciative have thanked me for my service. In airports it is almost impossible for a service member to pay for their own meal. Their support and appreciation is heartfelt, earnest, and genuine. However, I am left with a distinct impression that while individual citizens may understand, America does not. The war is not real at home. It touches the country only through a perilously thin connection to a generation of men and women who have chosen to insulate our country from the darkness that presses relentlessly at our borders.

So, if I were asked again the question "Are we winning?" I would have to say "Yes!" War has not descended upon America and almost everything I value is safe. Are the Iraqis winning? I will have to go back and see. There is absolutely no way to know given the abject failure of our news media. I pray that they are; I have too many friends there now to wish anything else. Which brings us to the most important question, "Is it worth the cost?" For the nation, absolutely. For several hundred thousand of my brothers in arms? I will not be so bold as to speak for them; each will have to decide for himself. For me? I will not know until I win custody of my girls.

Until then, I have a plane to board, more friends to see, and a team to bring home.

Update #27: 12 November 2007— On Parade

Daylight Savings had kicked in, so while it was not late, it was very dark and my body still had not recovered from the five days of travel and waiting it took to get back from Kansas to my team. I dozed off, waking as I felt the helicopter begin its rapid drop into the LZ. I had no clue if this was my stop or not, several of us occupied the lead ship en route to various remote locations. I could make out the distinct outlines of a military installation below, and in the distance, a small town. The bird settled in a storm of dust, the crew chief dismounting with practiced ease, slid open the troop door and pointed to me and one other. "Numiniyah?" I yelled over the din of the rotors. Thumbs up. Releasing my harness and grabbing my bags, I jumped out. Seconds later the birds were gone.

Major Koast moved out onto the airstrip and grabbed a bag. We exchanged the typical welcome home from leave rituals, which had now become all too familiar. I was the last to go, so my return marked a milestone in the team's history. The end was in sight. A short ride took us to the compound where my four teams and our National Police brigade lived.

For several months, we anticipated taking the brigade to a month-long training course at the Numiniyah National Police Training Academy. The program was established about eighteen months ago as a reaction to the rampant corruption that plagued the entire National Police organization. The idea was to bring each brigade out of the battle, get rid of the corrupt leaders, and then put them through a rigorous curriculum of ethics, police skills, and tactical training. At the end of the training, each unit would receive the new blue digital pattern National Police uniform, and the brigade would return to the fight, hopefully with a renewed sense of nationalism and without the militia influences that plagued them. The entire process became known as "re-bluing."

My brigade had originally planned to go to Numiniyah and re-blue back in June. A combination of good performance and success in Karkh by Brigadier General Bahaa's men and some very poor performance in other areas of the city led to a series of shifts. Other brigades moved forward in the timeline and we kept shifting to the right on the calendar. Eventually there was no other brigade to switch us with. With all the political importance swirling around the September Congressional hearings and enemy activities down in Karbala, the 5th Brigade's September rotation was cancelled as well. When I left for leave, it looked like we might be the only brigade not to go at all. The day after I left, however, orders came down and my team packed the brigade up and moved them south.

It is both satisfying and humbling to return to your unit and find that everything is running full steam ahead without you. I got a quick tour of the facilities, an introduction to the Australian cadre, warm greetings from the team, and then a much-needed cup of chai and a happy reunion with the General. The training had been going very well, and over the next few days, it was increasingly obvious that the brigade had benefited enormously. We still shake our collective heads at much of what we see and have all but given up in making headway in some areas that western forces deem important. But, by and large, they were looking more and more like soldiers.

I returned in time to see the last few days of the standard curriculum and just in time to partake in the end of course culmination tactical exercise and the all-important graduation parade practice. Apparently General Bahaa had been drilling his eighteen hundred shurta for a few hours every afternoon. The familiar art of the parade field connects armies of every culture and every generation in a way that probably no other activity can. The specifics of arm swing, pace count, or angle of the hand salute may vary, but the focus on attention to detail, precision and perfection persists.

"If you are taller than the man in front of you, move up!"

"You're out of step Mohammed!"

"Swing your arms Mustafa, all the way up to the shoulder of the man in front."

Lines painted on the parade ground mark precisely where commanders, flag bearers and musicians will stand. Officers and a precious few NCOs swarm around each formation making corrections.

Several days before graduation the shurta received two sets of the new blue uniforms. They are the last brigade to get them, and they are anxious. They discard a wild menagerie of old army green and desert uniforms issued from various American programs over the last few years or purchased from markets. Camouflage patterns from Jordan, Egypt, Russia, the United Kingdom, the U.S., or the former Iraqi Army, all discarded in a heap and replaced by one standard. There is something remarkably transforming about issuing a young man a uniform and lining him up with thousands of his countrymen all dedicated to the same purpose. The exact same energy generals like Napoleon harnessed to draft class after class of Frenchmen to perform his will. The next day's parade was an entirely transformed affair. Shurta stood taller, paid more attention, marched straighter. An organization, which a week earlier looked like a militia, now looked like an army.

There is something about parades and ceremonies that make General Officers minds' race. They all seem to have a "good idea fairy" land on their shoulder and whisper in their ears. Brigadier General Bahaa decided they needed white gloves and sent his commanders out to find some. Eighteen hundred white gloves in a land without power; I shook my head. And, that was before I heard the solution - medical gloves. One of the shurta suggested they use the white latex medical gloves that our medics used while treating them and training them in first aid skills. I do not tell the General "no" often, but I drew the line here. "Sir, I don't have them, and I am not going to go find them." Somehow, the Second Battalion all showed up on parade day in latex gloves. If only they had kept them for the following day when it came time to clean out their nasty barracks.

The month had been good for the brigade and for my four teams. Life in Baghdad had become routine, and many of my guys had become frustrated by a lack of progress. The opportunity to train, and more importantly to show the Iraqis the value of training, was invaluable. It was also good to get the Iraqis off the street corners and out of harm's way for a while. The compound we lived in was spartan. Eight three-story buildings surrounding a central courtyard and a motor pool, all enclosed in barbed wire. While the Americans and Australian cadre had free reign, the Iraqis, had been disarmed, had their cell phones removed, and were pretty strictly controlled. An untrained observer could have easily concluded that he was looking at a prison camp. However, the atmosphere was remarkably festive in the evenings with Iraqis huddling in small groups, smoking, singing, and dancing. A series of unit vs. unit soccer games and other competitions provided entertainment. The final match saw the defeat of the joint American-Aussie team by a composite team of the Iraqis, ending the season in good form. I think the final score was 4-2. We were happy with that, having expected a rout.

Figure 47: Training at Numiniya

Figure 48: Graduation Parade

Graduation came and went with the usual delegation of dignitaries there to observe. It was followed immediately by the race to clear the barracks and to line up the convoys for the trip home. The brigade had earned a week of leave, so many of them departed directly from the academy for homes across Iraq. Those who lived in Baghdad mounted trucks to get the brigade's equipment home. We approached the outskirts of Baghdad as the sun set. As we wound through the eastern part of the city, it became common for one truck or another to pull over to the side of the road and kick a grinning shurta out of the cab with his buddies waving and singing as he wandered off into his neighborhood. We crossed the bridge over the Tigris and back into Karkh at the south end of Haifa Street. It had been almost a month since I had left. It was good to be home.

Over the next few days, we reintegrated with our Coalition Headquarters and caught up on all that we had missed and the various plans in development that would affect or immediate future. Our district had continued to make progress while we had been gone. U.S. forces had finally captured the main criminal on Haifa Street, who had eluded capture for months, several days prior. Arresting Hussein Hani provided a bit of closure for all of us who had worked so hard to end his intimidation and thuggery. With both the Sunni and Shia threats largely defeated in our sector, I feel pretty good about the future of the district. Other bad actors will inevitably move in to try to start trouble, but their task will be much harder now that the old established gangs have been broken.

It became increasingly clear over the next few days that we would not be staying in Karkh. Brigadier General Bahaa and his brigade's reputation had gotten them noticed. Fresh out of training, he was essentially unemployed. The Minister of Defense and Minister of Interior both had competing demands, and the political struggle to determine where Brigadier General Bahaa would be committed next began in earnest.

In what had become a disturbing pattern, I was spending all my American holidays with senior Iraqi leaders. I spent July 4th with Brigadier General Bahaa and Major General Hussein discussing poetry and trying to keep Brigadier General Bahaa out of jail. Four months later, I spent Veterans Day with Brigadier General Bahaa and Major General Hussein cooling our heels discussing passport reform with a Deputy Minister of the Interior while we waited to go see the Minister about our next mission. MOD and MOI had issued conflicting guidance and we needed answers. After several hours, Brigadier General Bahaa and Major General Hussein were ushered into the Minister's office. A phone call to the Prime Minister sealed the deal. They cut orders. Brigadier General Bahaa apparently mentioned to the Minister of the Interior that I was outside, so the Minister invited me in. Every other time we had met, the Minister had been in a huge hurry and completely uninterested in an American lieutenant colonel. He apparently had a light schedule that night and sat us all down for chai. He rattled off a whole string of questions about our training at Numiniyah and the performance of the National Police and my impressions of Baghdad. I have many impressions … more than he had chai. As we left, he wished me a happy Veterans Day, and thanked me for my service to his country. Needless to say, I was impressed. On the way out, he reiterated our new orders to the generals. Our final month may be interesting.

Once more into the breach.

Update #28: 22 November 2007— They Have Room For Me

"Gunner, Sabot, two Hinds, left hind first, driver move up."

"Where?'

"200 mils left of TRP#2, just over the barn … driver stop."

"Identified."

"Fire."

"On the way."

KABOOM

"Target, right Hind."

"Identified."

"Flashing zeros – relaze….Fire!

"On the way…"

KARACK

"Target, Cease fire, driver back up."

The sound track of my youth played over in my head. As a young lieutenant, we practiced tank engagements against Soviet tanks and helicopters over and over again. I spent countless hours in the Unit Conduct of Fire Trainer (UCOFT), which is a huge, over-grown tank gunnery computer game. My crews killed thousands of computer generated Soviet HIND-D attack helicopters.

Fifteen years later, I followed Brigadier General Bahaa on a foot patrol in the northwest suburbs of Ad Diwaniyah, a mid-sized town in southern Iraq. My HMMWVs shadowed us several hundred meters behind providing overwatch. The Apache gunships that had been circling overhead all morning had broken station for fuel several minutes before. I heard the new birds long before I saw them, the low buildings on either side of the street masking the horizon. Then the beast appeared. The HIND-D is an ugly brutish bird, far larger than our own more agile craft. Designed to carry both a huge weapons payload and troops in the lead of a Soviet armored column, it is quite literally a flying tank. It cleared the rooftops and came straight at us, its twin following shortly after in its trail.

My heart beat faster in spite of myself. This Polish aircraft was on my side now, and its near constant presence in the sky above the city served as a significant deterrent to enemy rocket and mortar activity during daylight hours. I could not help but feel several decades out of place. On foot, patrolling with Iraqi light infantry, calling in close air support from Polish attack helicopters … I would not have dreamed it in a thousand years.

After just a few days back in Baghdad from our training, we were once again ordered south. The town of Ad Diwaniyah is the provincial capital of one of Iraq's southern districts and lies in the heart of the Multi-National Division's area. The region is largely Shia, and while it has not felt much of the Sunni-Shia violence, it has recently become more volatile as the Shia factions increasingly fight amongst themselves for political gain. My 5th Brigade of National Police got tossed into that mix to both Brigadier General Bahaa's and my dissatisfaction. "Ours is not to wonder why …" goes the famous poem.

The trip south was remarkably easy. Brigadier General Bahaa's battalions settled into various governmental compounds around the city and my team carved out a spot in FOB Echo. A no-nonsense Polish Major General currently commands the Multi-National Division. A battalion of Poles, a battalion of Romanians, and a battalion from Mongolia make up the bulk of the force in the city with a smattering of five other nations that are represented in varying degrees. American officers augment the staff. African guards staff the private security company that runs much of the base security. A few young Asian girls from Kyrghistan staff the Green Bean Coffee shop. The sister of one of them lives in the trailer next to me up in FOB Prosperity – small world. Iraqi nationals work the laundry. Pakistanis work the mess hall.

British and Australian contractors work various repair facilities. The motor pools are an armored vehicle enthusiast's playground.

Brigadier General Bahaa is eager to get to work. The National Police have a long-term agenda to move out of Baghdad to take on the roll it was created for and work the outlying districts. Several brigades have been sent out before with some mixed results. Brigadier General Bahaa is anxious to prove that his Brigade, fresh out of training, is up to the task. The local Army commanders are wary. They did not ask for more forces - the Minister of Interior forced the 5th Brigade upon them. After two days, they grudgingly give Brigadier General Bahaa a task.

He executes with characteristic vigor. His shurta are impressive. His officers and NCOs have rid the ranks of all the old uniforms, and for a change, every man has a helmet and body armor. The new uniforms have done wonders for the formation. They look impressive and disciplined. A local unit of emergency police is married up with them for the operation. The locals wear the ragtag smattering of mixed uniforms and face masks that were our lot a few short weeks ago. They look like ill-disciplined thugs and act like it. The Brigade notices it and stands a bit taller.

The first day's operation goes very well. Eighteen detainees and eighty assorted weapons are pulled from a neighborhood that was supposedly "safe." We spend the afternoon doing foot patrols around areas that Coalition Forces do not normally enter. We are greeted warmly wherever we go. We have packed 1600 troops into a very small area. It is impressive. The locals take note. So do the local politicians. Fifteen of the eighteen detainees work for one of the local bigwigs. They were not supposed to be captured nor are they supposed to be armed. Brigadier General Bahaa could not give a damn about local politics and detains them anyway. That night we get orders that would put us in a small town about an hour to the east early the next morning. We are told it is where "all of the enemy fled" when the operation started.

We swarm the small village of Afak the next morning. By noon, it is clear we are on a wild goose chase. We think it was deliberate. The locals greet us enthusiastically. The day is bright and clear and we spend mid-morning eating falafel at a local stand and drinking chai with the village elders in the city square. We walk off our lunch with a patrol. A small stream divides the town, with palms lining parks on either side. We cross over a footbridge and into a covered market. Life in Afak is quiet and largely untouched by the violence of the north. The shops are well stocked and the people are happy. One of my team's terps has family from Afak. They call him later to tell them how the locals were impressed by the professionalism and behavior of the brigade. A year ago the arrival of a National Police brigade would have spread terror.

For several more days, we conducted operations on the periphery of the main operations going on in town. Brigadier General Bahaa was understandably frustrated. I took a slightly different view—maybe because I am getting short and am ready to hand off my baton. This series of relatively easy missions was good for the brigade. It built confidence, allowed them to practice what they had learned, and left them with a good reputation. Eventually, the political charade ended and the brigade received orders back to Baghdad. They had a new mission—a new part of the city to occupy. The scrimmages are over and a new season is about to begin.

Figure 49: MAJ Hamid (5-2NP Adjutant), Lieutenant Colonel Hussein (2-5-2NP Commander), Brigadier General Bahaa (5-2NP Commander), COL Mohammad (5-2NP Deputy Commander), Lieutenant Colonel Ashan (3-5-2NP Commander), Lieutenant Colonel Abdullah (2-5-2NP Deputy Commander) Captain Mundar (5-2NP Personal Security Detachment Commander)

We made it back to Baghdad in time for Thanksgiving. I found myself spending the morning drinking chai with Major General Hussein, the National Police Commander. We talk about the new mission and his favorite singer whose song plays on the TV. We talk about the Christian church service in Dora he attended at St. Josephs the day before. It was the first time a service was held there in ages. He had not been there in years, but reminisced about various Iraqi Christian friends buried there. We talk about Thanksgiving. I joke with him that I spend all the American holidays with him and ask him for a photo I can take with me so he can be with me at Christmas. He chuckled, and then looks at his watch. "Lieutenant Colonel Green, come with me, I have a meeting." I look at my own watch. Brigadier General Bahaa is now forty minutes late and I am about to get dragged into a meeting that is not the one I came for. Major General Hussein has my hand now and drags me along out of his office. I find Brigadier General Bahaa waiting in the hall.

"Saydee, what are you doing out here?"

"Lieutenant Colonel Green, what were you doing in there with my boss?"

I laugh. "Telling stories about you!"

Major General Hussein shuffles us both into a conference room. He sits at the head of the table. A smattering of National Police sergeants fills all the other seats at the main table. I find a seat in the back row, as does Brigadier General Bahaa and his deputy Colonel Mohammad. This is very odd - the Iraqi National Police has an almost non-existent Non-Commissioned Officer corps—and they damn sure do not sit at the big boy table while officers sit in the back row. My curiosity is peaked. I count heads. Thirteen. One for each of the National Police Divisions and Brigades. It becomes quickly apparent that each sergeant represents one of those commands. I recognized Arif Awol Amir from my own brigade. We have been working with limited success to build up his authority as a sergeant for months.

Major General Hussein begins to speak. I love listening to him, in the way that a kid listens to a grandfather. He speaks very softly and slowly. His thoughts often trail off. He repeats himself often. However, he peppers his thoughts with anecdotes and stories and quotes, so I am naturally drawn to him. He begins by telling the assembly about the very first Battalion Command Sergeant Major he met when he was a lieutenant in the old Iraqi Army. He recalled every detail of the man. Then he told of his first platoon sergeant, a man who became a close friend and died many years later in a car accident. He talked of old military traditions: changing of the guard, raising the colors in the morning, and lowering them at night. He talked of inspections, and standards, and NCOs that new every man by name. He lamented the death of those traditions as his country suffered through the era of Saddam, the Iran-Iraq war, Desert Storm and the following embargo. Over the next hour, he challenged those thirteen non-commissioned officers to go back to their brigades and give a new birth to that old tradition. Time will tell if that spark will ignite the fire of change. If it does, it will have been an historic moment for the Iraqi National Police. I was a bit humbled to have stumbled into the event.

Major General Hussein made one other comment that stuck with me. He told the NCOs that he was going to send them deliberately outside the country for training. To any training or to any foreign military school that he could find regardless of subject. Not for the training's sake, but to get them to see the rest of the world. "As a child" he said, "I was always told that Iraq was the most advanced and cultured of the Arab countries and that all the others were mere Bedouins." He went on to describe a trip two years ago to Oman, where he expected to find nothing but Bedouins and instead found a thriving modern nation which blended east and west and had far surpassed Iraq. For thirty-five years Sadaam had kept the Iraqi people isolated. While they had stagnated, the rest of the world had flourished. "I had become the Bedouin," he lamented. "I am going to send you out into the world so that you can take your culture to it and you can find culture to bring back to Iraq."

Compare that vision with the alternatives offered by Osama Bin Laden. Progress in Iraq is not fast, but leaders of character are slowly emerging and leading change.

Figure 50: Major General Hussein, COL Roberts, Brigadier General Bahaa, and Lieutenant Colonel Green eat at the National Police Headquarters

I sat in an internet café down at FOB Echo last week. The free Morale and Welfare Recreational Services café was packed and the connection was far too slow. I had escaped over to the Iraqi run shop and paid a small fee. It was thick with cigarette smoke and filled with the noise of a soccer match. The local terp crowd and international soldiers frequented it far more than the U.S. troopers did. A thirty-something female terp sat at the terminal next to me. Western clothes and a headscarf put her in the moderately conservative camp. Some female terps abandon their eastern ways altogether, and a precious few cling to them completely. Age appears to be the most prevalent determining factor in which style they choose. The young woman clicked away for several minutes and then all of a sudden, she yelled in triumph "THEY HAVE ROOM FOR ME!" She shrieked and giggled and cried and spun around and danced all at once. Then she ran out of the room into the night yelling in a mix of Arabic and English, "I must go tell them at once!"

I could not help myself, and glanced at her screen left untouched in her euphoric exit. An official memorandum from the U.S. Department of Immigration informed her that her Visa application was approved! She returned several minutes later, followed by a steady stream of other young Iraqis and a few of the Americans she worked with. Each took a moment to read the document and share in her joy. Lady Liberty's light could not have shown brighter than the glow from the computer monitor that night.

As I sit in my hooch this Thanksgiving, I cannot help but feel thankful to come from a nation whose promise is so wonderful after all these years that people from vastly different cultures still look to it and decide that, sight unseen, they will make a leap of faith and risk everything to move there. No other nation has ever held that power over others.

"They have room for me!"

Update #29: 7 December 2007— Change of Mission

It gets dark early these days, like the end of a movie when everything fades to black. Driving the dimly lit stretch of Route Jackson back north to the International Zone, I half expect to see the credits start rolling up my windshield and the orchestra striking up for the grand finale.

I hate endings. Always have. I hate the end of a really good book, one whose characters I have come to know. I hate the ending of a song; I can never remember how they go. I hate graduations, funerals, retirements, and goodbyes. I hate knowing that something that I have invested my heart in is no longer there for me to fuss over. I hate feeling irrelevant.

That is exactly how the days since our return from Diwaniyah have felt. The brigade has orders to a new sector, one that is both much bigger and will have many more forces for Brigadier General Bahaa to control. There are new Coalition forces to build relationships with, new council members and sheiks and Imams, new streets, shops, and parks. New children and new criminals. I sit next to Brigadier General Bahaa and admire his new carpets, adorning a much larger office. The map on the wall is of an area of responsibility that is not mine and will not be. I take no interest in it. Officers from new Iraqi and American units sit across from me in familiar couches. I take no interest in them either. All of it belongs to a story that is not mine to tell. And, in an odd way I am jealous because the new author will be borrowing many of my characters. Characters who I have grown to care for, far more than I would have thought, and far too much to entrust to anyone else.

So with the jealousy goes a tinge of guilt. I get to escape free, safe, unharmed and with nothing left to risk. While Brigadier General Bahaa, Mohammad, Hamid, Hassan, Ali, Nabil, Safah, Faras, Husein, Mundar, Mahmoud and countless others are left to carry on the struggle. Never mind that it is their homeland and not mine. Never mind that the root causes of much of the struggle grows from a religion that I cannot give any credence to, and political rivalries about which I have no vested interest. Somehow, the task had become ours and to leave without an assured outcome leaves a void.

Not everyone on my team feels that way. Some convinced themselves the time was wasted—a year of their lives they will never get back. While they have served both honorably and well, they failed to internalize any of it. They will laugh at me for using the word "failed." For them, the ability to leave it all behind will be a victory of its own. Who knows, maybe they are far more sane than I am. It is hard to measure exactly what we accomplished. We went to war and never fired a shot. We were in the vicinity of danger but never personally attacked. We have attended some significant meetings but were not the key players. We have coached but not played. It has been a strange war.

I hope that in the days to come, when their own children's laughter once again fills their ears, when the smell of a lover's hair delights their senses, when they sit on family farms, or in a hometown park, or eat quietly at a favorite restaurant, when all of the frustration and fatigue, and stress and fear have finally faded…I hope they can look back and see that their efforts really did make a tangible difference in the life of a nation.

I am proud of our brigade - my brigade. A year ago, when we fought our way into the slums of Haifa Street, down unlit and neglected roads, we were an armed rabble with a dubious reputation. In many cases, only the presence of my team served to convince the much-abused people that the 5th Brigade was anything other than an extension of the nightmare the sectarian militias had unleashed upon the city. Today, the Sword Brigade's reputation precedes it. Neighborhoods are welcoming them, confident and hopeful –expecting that good things will come to them as well.

I am proud of my friend Brigadier General Bahaa Noori Yaseen. It has been a privilege to watch him take command and so dramatically change his unit. I was sent here with the specified task of providing him training, coaching and mentoring. I leave with very little doubt that I received far more than I gave. I have watched him make some of the hardest moral and ethical choices I have seen anyone confronted with. I have seen him stand up to political pressure, which would bend all but the most principled men. I have seen him make mistakes and learn from them. I have heard him say "I told you so," and "I am sorry." We have taken some incredibly stupid risks together. We have witnessed things I do not care to see again. We have celebrated, laughed and cried. I had always wanted a big brother and never dreamed I might find one here in Iraq.

Our replacements have arrived. They are full of all the cocky youthful vigor that one would expect. I am certain we were just the same. They are anxious to take over, and we are having a hard time letting go. The first of my guys was dropped off at the airport today, waiting to start the journey home. The rest will filter out over the next few days. The terps are shaken up. So are we. Victor, Frank, Rafid, and Al have been through much with us. They must start making connections with the new team, but are all eagerly awaiting the VISA applications that will let them catch up to us. The team is slowly breaking apart, and within a few short weeks will have made the long journey home and scatter to the winds. The final verse of the famous WWI poem "In Flanders Fields" echoes in my head.

Take up our quarrel with the foe:
To you from failing hands we throw
The torch; be yours to hold it high.
If ye break faith with us who die
We shall not sleep, though poppies grow
In Flanders fields.

It is time for me to come home. I look forward to winter's chill and the promise of spring and new beginnings.

Afterward

It is summer again, but it hardly feels that way. Baghdad's heat no longer intrudes. I am thankful. Weekends are spent at the lake and not in the streets. Explosives mark the end of celebrations like the Fourth of July and not the beginning of a long hard day.

Six months have disappeared in the blink of an eye. My team returned home to Fort Riley on 17 Dec 2007 and spent a few days out-processing before being released to our families and the rest of our lives. We scattered back from whence we came to reunite with loved ones. In some cases to pick up exactly where we left off, and in others to move on to new assignments around the Army. An occasional email or phone call charts the progress of vacations, the selling of a house, the birth of a baby, or the expectation of a new one. Every now and again, a note in broken English will update us on our terps and the world we left behind.

I returned to a battle for which I was completely untrained—divorce. Mercifully, a host of allies; friends, family, and neighbors came to my aid, and by spring, I had full custody of my daughters. The Army has taken care of it's own, and I have an assignment that lets me concentrate on being a father again. Together at last, the three of us thrive in ways I would never have anticipated.

When I go back and read my final letter, I note that it is filled with far more questions than answers. That seems even more magnified now, as I become increasingly removed from the events of last year. News from Iraq continues to show progress with significant gains made as the result of the Awakening movements and legislative progress. The Iraqi Government has shown a new willingness to fight for a national rather than sectarian agenda and has openly engaged the powerful Jesh Al-Mahdi militia in Basra and in Sadr City.

But the specific news is scarce. I know that Brigadier General Bahaa is still in command of the 5th Brigade but I have been unable to judge how effective he has been in his new area of responsibility. Many of his staff were reassigned after we left, and many of our terps left the team for other positions or in anticipation of approved visa requests. The Blackjack Brigade came home a few months after my team, so I have lost the contacts that let me gauge what has happened on Haifa Street or in the neighborhoods that were the central focus of this story. I keep my eyes open for anything that might give me a hint.

I expect it will take years or more to fully understand how the events of 2007 shaped Iraq. It may take far longer to come to any consensus on the value of the outcome which is still uncertain. I remain optimistic.

Printed in the United States
128876LV00007B/24/P